PROTAGONIST

The
Seedbed
Daily Text

PROTAGONIST

Stepping into the Story of Advent

Advent

MATT LEROY & JOSH LEROY

Unless otherwise indicated, all Scripture quotations are taken from the Holy Bible, New International Version®, NIV®. Copyright © 1973, 1978, 1984, 2011 by Biblica, Inc.™ Used by permission of Zondervan. All rights reserved worldwide. www.zondervan.com The "NIV" and "New International Version" are trademarks registered in the United States Patent and Trademark Office by Biblica, Inc.™

Scripture quotations marked NRSV are from New Revised Standard Version Bible, copyright © 1989 National Council of the Churches of Christ in the United States of America. Used by permission. All rights reserved.

Printed in the United States of America

Cover and page design by Strange Last Name
Page layout by PerfecType, Nashville, Tennessee

LeRoy, Matthew.
  Protagonist : stepping into the story of Advent / Matt Leroy & Josh Leroy. – Franklin, Tennessee : Seedbed Publishing, ©2019.

        pages ; cm. – (Seedbed daily text)

        ISBN 9781628245929 (paperback)
        ISBN 9781628245936 (Mobi)
        ISBN 9781628245943 (ePub)
        ISBN 9781628247077 (uPDF)

        1. Advent--Meditations.
        I. LeRoy, Joshua. II. Title. III. Series.

BV40.L476 2019   242.33   2019948933

SEEDBED PUBLISHING
Franklin, Tennessee
seedbed.com

Contents

How the Daily Text Works

It seems obvious to say . . . but the Daily Text is written every day. Mostly, it is written the day before it is scheduled to release online.

Before we go further, I would like to cordially invite you to subscribe and receive the daily e-mail. Visit seedbed.com /dailytext to get started. Also check out the popular Facebook group, Seedbed Daily Text.

Eventually, the daily postings become part of a Daily Text discipleship resource. That's what you hold in your hands now.

It's not exactly a Bible study, though the Bible is both the source and subject. You will learn something about the Bible along the way: its history, context, original languages, and authors. The goal is not educational in nature but transformational. We are more interested in knowing Jesus than knowing *about* Jesus.

To that end, each reading begins with the definitive inspiration of the Holy Spirit, the ongoing, unfolding text of Scripture. Following the scripture is a short and, hopefully, substantive insight from the text and some aspect of its meaning. For insight to lead to deeper influence, we turn the text into prayer. Finally, influence must run its course toward impact. That is why we ask each other questions. The questions are not designed to elicit information but to crystallize intention.

Discipleship always leads from inspiration to intention and from attention to action.

Using the Daily Text as a Discipleship Curricular Resource for Groups

While Scripture always addresses us personally, it is not written to us individually. The content of Scripture cries out for a community to address. The Daily Text is made for discipleship in community. This resource can work in several different ways. It could be read like a traditional book, a few pages or chapters at a time. Though unadvisable, the readings could be crammed in on the night before the meeting. Keep in mind, the Daily Text is not called the Daily Text for kicks. We believe Scripture is worthy of our most focused and consistent attention. Every day. We all have misses, but let's make every day more than a noble aspiration. Let's make it our covenant with one another.

For Use with Bands

In our judgment, the best and highest use of the Daily Text is made through what we call banded discipleship. A discipleship band is a same-gender group of three to five people who read together, pray together, and meet together to become the love of God for one another and the world. With banded discipleship, the daily readings serve more as a common text for the band and grist for the interpersonal conversation mill between meetings. The band meeting is reserved for the specialized activities of high-bar discipleship.

To learn more about bands and banded discipleship, visit discipleshipbands.com. Be sure to download the free *Discipleship Bands: A Practical Field Guide* or order a supply of the printed booklets online. Also, be sure to explore Discipleship Bands, our native app designed specifically for the practice of banded discipleship, in the Apple store or at Google Play.

For Use with Classes and Small Groups

The Daily Text has also proven to be a helpful discipleship resource for a variety of small groups, from community groups to Sunday school classes. Here are some suggested guidelines for deploying the Daily Text as a resource for a small group or class setting:

I. Hearing the Text

Invite the group to settle into silence for a period of no less than one and no more than five minutes. Ask an appointed person to keep time and to read the biblical text covering the period of days since the last group meeting. Allow at least one minute of silence following the reading of the text.

II. Responding to the Text

Invite anyone from the group to respond to the reading by answering these prompts: What did you hear? What did you see? What did you otherwise sense from the Lord?

III. Sharing Insights and Implications for Discipleship

Moving in an orderly rotation (or free-for-all), invite people to share insights and implications from the week's readings. What did you find challenging, encouraging, provocative, comforting, invasive, inspiring, corrective, affirming, guiding, or warning? Allow group conversation to proceed at will. Limit to one sharing item per turn, with multiple rounds of discussion.

IV. Shaping Intentions for Prayer

Invite each person in the group to share a single discipleship intention for the week ahead. It is helpful if the intention can also be framed as a question the group can use to check in from the prior week. At each person's turn, he or she is invited to share how their intention went during the previous week. The class or group can open and close their meeting according to their established patterns.

Introduction

Advent means arrival. It is a word we often associate with the arrival of some life-changing technology. And often these inventions are hailed for advancing our great cultural obsession: the elimination of waiting. With each innovation, we attempt to expedite the process in the name of progress and rush more of the world to our fingertips. We thought this would create time, but we seem to be losing more of it and losing touch with it.

In the kingdom imagination, however, Advent tells an alternative story. It is a season in the Christian calendar in which we intentionally enter into a time of waiting, longing for the arrival of Jesus at Christmas. What you hold in your hands is a guide through that season, a humble attempt to root us in an ancient rhythm of time and push against the tide of hurry. This book provides Scripture, reflections, prayer, and questions for each day through Advent, into the twelve days of Christmas known as Christmastide, and culminating at Epiphany.

Resisting the urge to rush ahead to the Nativity, we engage with the countercultural, subversive practice of pilgrimage. We sink down into the ancient story of God's people and remember what it means to hope. We walk with them on the desert road and look to the heavens for help. We ache and thrill with the Prophets. We sing along with the Poets. And when the Promise arrives at last in shocking glory, we rejoice at the grace we still can't get our minds and hearts around.

PROTAGONIST

The Protagonist

JOHN 1:1–5, 14–18 | In the beginning was the Word, and the Word was with God, and the Word was God. He was with God in the beginning. Through him all things were made; without him nothing was made that has been made. In him was life, and that life was the light of all mankind. The light shines in the darkness, and the darkness has not overcome it. . . .

The Word became flesh and made his dwelling among us. We have seen his glory, the glory of the one and only Son, who came from the Father, full of grace and truth.

(John testified concerning him. He cried out, saying, "This is the one I spoke about when I said, 'He who comes after me has surpassed me because he was before me.'") Out of his fullness we have all received grace in place of grace already given. For the law was given through Moses; grace and truth came through Jesus Christ. No one has ever seen God, but the one and only Son, who is himself God and is in closest relationship with the Father, has made him known.

Consider This

Hamlet could never meet Shakespeare.

C. S. Lewis once made this observation, pointing out that William Shakespeare knew all there was to know about Hamlet, the character he invented. His motivations, his fears, his hopes. Shakespeare put the words in his mouth and the paths beneath his feet and the shape to his world. And the character could experience the creator through the echoes of his voice in every line of dialogue, his fingerprints on every detail of the setting. Yet the character could never break out of the play or move off of the page and into the world of the playwright. Hamlet could never meet Shakespeare.

Unless, of course, the author wrote himself into the story.

If the creator made himself one of the characters, if he scripted himself into the play, then he could make himself known to the cast. He could be heard, seen, touched by them. Then, and only then, could Hamlet meet Shakespeare.

Every analogy breaks down somewhere, and any analogy about God caves in at an accelerated pace. But this is a hint toward the mystery of the incarnation. During this season of Advent, we long for the arrival of Jesus at Christmas. We wait with hopeful anticipation for him to step into the story. Bound by our sin and locked in our fallen world with no way to break ourselves out, reconciliation with God was an impossible dream. We could never get to him. Our only hope is that he comes to us. And in the fullness of time, the plot takes a scandalous turn, that we dared not even imagine.

The Creator steps into the story, and takes on the lead role.

The Author becomes the Protagonist.

"All the world's a stage," the bard once wrote.

And the one who built the theater and crafted the script prepares to make his entrance.

The Prayer

Jesus, center of every story, we wait for you.

The Questions

- Who is the lead character of your story?
- How did Jesus make his entrance into your story?

AND THE WORD BECAME FLESH,
AND MADE HIS DWELLING AMONG US.

Let There Be Light

2

GENESIS 1:1–5 | In the beginning God created the heavens and the earth. Now the earth was formless and empty, darkness was over the surface of the deep, and the Spirit of God was hovering over the waters.

And God said, "Let there be light," and there was light. God saw that the light was good, and he separated the light from the darkness. God called the light "day," and the darkness he called "night." And there was evening, and there was morning—the first day.

Consider This

Creation began in the dark.
But piercing the black void of nothingness,
God's voice rings out,

Let there be light
Let there be day and night
Let there be earth and sky
Land and sea
Mountain and valley
And river and forest
Let there be life to fill it all
And then, the crown of creation,
Let there be humanity
Let them be in our image
Let them be the glory of God walking the earth
Let us be at one, in harmony, together.
And we answer,
Let there be pride
Let there be betrayal and rebellion
Let there be separation
Let there be sin and death and fall.

Now, I know what you're thinking. That's a pretty depressing way to start the Christmas season. But, in truth, it's the only way to start. This is how Advent orients us into the larger story. Refusing to let us run ahead, charging us to pause long enough to remember. We must begin by remembering our sin, our need for rescue, our desperate longing for a Savior.

Pastor and writer Fleming Rutledge reminds us, "Advent begins in the dark."[1]

---

1. This is an often-repeated theme in Fleming Rutledge's collection of Advent sermons entitled *Advent: The Once and Future Coming of Jesus* (Grand Rapids: Wm. B. Eerdmans Publishing Co., 2018).

At the outset of this season of light we sink down into the darkness of exile, sense the looming shadow of death, long for the light like Israel of old. Like captives waiting for deliverance. Like runaways and rebels hoping for a return.

Wait and hope are the twin anthems of Advent. It's interesting that in both Hebrew and Latin, the root word for "wait" can also be translated as "hope." A reminder that we do not despair as we wait in the darkness. But we light a lone candle, the first flame of hope, pushing back the shadow one spark at a time.

Advent begins in the dark. But around the edges of the deep horizon we see a faded gray creeping in. We hear a forgotten, yet familiar voice.

The people living in darkness
Have seen a great light.
Let there be light
Again.

The Prayer

Light of the world, make me a new creation in you.

The Questions

- What has darkness looked like for you?
- How did the light break through?

AND THE WORD BECAME FLESH,
AND MADE HIS DWELLING AMONG US.

3 Christmas, Come Down

ISAIAH 64:1–4 | Oh, that you would rend the heavens and come down, that the mountains would tremble before you! As when fire sets twigs ablaze and causes water to boil, come down to make your name known to your enemies and cause the nations to quake before you! For when you did awesome things that we did not expect, you came down, and the mountains trembled before you. Since ancient times no one has heard, no ear has perceived, no eye has seen any God besides you, who acts on behalf of those who wait for him.

Consider This

Oh, that you would rend the heavens and come down.

These are the words of Isaiah, the prophet laureate of Advent. We hang on his words this time every year, waiting for the arrival of the promised Savior. And no one casts that vision quite like Isaiah. But here in chapter 64 of his book, he breaks from the familiar tones of expectant hope and instead pours out a lament.

To "rend a garment" in ancient Jewish culture was a sign of deep despair and mourning, an outward physical representation of what was taking place in the soul. In this lament Isaiah draws on this imagery as he pleads for God to mourn with us, to "rend the heavens" like a garment. Look at the chaos of the world, Lord, and grieve alongside us.

But Isaiah asks for more. Don't just grieve over what is wrong, come down and set it right. Don't just share our pain; be active in healing it. We need a theophany, an appearance, a sighting that we can get our senses around. We know you are working behind the scenes, directing the play. But we need you to step onto center stage and take the lead role.

And this, of course, is exactly what God does. God answers this prayer through the scandalous mystery of the incarnation. The Author steps into the story as the Protagonist. But not in the way that we expect.

We want the trembling mountains Isaiah describes in verse 1 or the blazing fire of verse 2. These images call to mind Moses on Mount Sinai or Elijah on Mount Carmel. We want to see that again! Instead, he moves more in line with the words of verse 3: "You did awesome things that we did not expect."

We want undeniable glory. He goes with the scandal of an unmarried pregnant teenager. We want the ground to shake. He comes as a baby. And, once again, we are reminded that Advent fulfills our greatest expectations in a way that we never expected.

The Prayer

O God, rend the heavens and come down.

The Questions

- Where do you need God to act in your life?

- How might he already be acting in unexpected ways?

AND THE WORD BECAME FLESH,
AND MADE HIS DWELLING AMONG US.

4 The Center of the Story

JEREMIAH 33:14–22 | "'The days are coming,' declares the LORD, 'when I will fulfill the good promise I made to the people of Israel and Judah. '"In those days and at that time I will make a righteous Branch sprout from David's line; he will do what is just and right in the land. In those days Judah will be saved and Jerusalem will live in safety. This is the name by which it will be called: The LORD Our Righteous Savior.' For this is what the LORD says: 'David will never fail to have a man to sit on the throne of Israel, nor will the Levitical priests ever fail to have a man to stand before me continually to offer burnt offerings, to burn grain offerings and to present sacrifices.'"

The word of the LORD came to Jeremiah: "This is what the LORD says: 'If you can break my covenant with the day and my covenant with the night, so that day and night no longer come at their appointed time, then my covenant with David my servant—and my covenant with the Levites who are priests ministering before me—can be broken and David will no longer have a descendant to reign on his throne. I will make the descendants of David my servant and the Levites who minister before me as countless as the stars in the sky and as measureless as the sand on the seashore.'"

Consider This

Of course, Jesus is fully God. We wholeheartedly proclaim his divinity and worship him for it. But in the incarnation he becomes fully human. And—perhaps there is more mystery here than we realize—he becomes a very particular kind of human.

In the Old Testament, God repeatedly makes covenant with the Jewish people. In this passage the prophet Jeremiah recounts these "good promise[s]" with echoes of the anchors of their history. He makes allusions to Adam and Eve, and the covenant with day and night established in the creation story. He sparks memories of Abraham and Sarah, pointing to the countless stars in the sky and measureless sand by the sea. And he explicitly speaks of the unrivaled reign of David and the Levitical law of Moses. He reminds us of the covenant movements through the grand sweep of Scripture. But in the days of fulfillment foreseen by Jeremiah, God does more than make a covenant with them. At the dawn of the New Testament, he becomes one of them.

We understand that Jesus was born for all people, but perhaps sometimes we forget that Jesus was born into a specific race of people, into a long cultural heritage and history. He carried distinct physical features (the tone of his skin, the color of his eyes, inherited family traits) that identified him with that people and he always fully embraced that identity. He was born into a race of people who had experienced hundreds of years of slavery, a trial they could never forget. He was born into a race of people who knew what it meant to be conquered by force. Repeatedly they were violently attacked and carried away from their homeland and into exile.

At the time of his birth, his people were living under the oppressive rule of the Roman Empire. The very dust beneath their feet had been promised to them by God himself. Yet Caesar, in all of his might, claimed it as his own and instituted a reign of systematic injustice. Taxes, laws, enforcement tactics—Jesus' people were at the mercy of the system. From the very first glance of his face and skin, from the very first sounds of his accent, from the things that he ate and the ways that he worshipped, it was undeniably clear that Jesus was firmly located and numbered among the oppressed. And that is exactly where he wanted to be. And that is exactly where we still find him.

The mystery of the incarnation will always baffle and amaze anyone who is even half awake. But perhaps it's this particular part of the mystery that is asking to be explored in days like these. To remember that ours is a story of a God who joins with the oppressed and shows up on the margins. Which transforms the margins from the forgotten edge of the page into the center of the whole story. He still invites us to seek him out and find him there. And more than that, to join him. Just as he has joined us.

The Prayer

God of the oppressed, God on the margins, draw me to where you are.

The Questions

- What does it mean to go to the margins in your community?
- What if Jesus is waiting for you there, among his people?

AND THE WORD BECAME FLESH,
AND MADE HIS DWELLING AMONG US.

Hope Is Always

5

PSALM 130:1–8 | Out of the depths I cry to you, LORD; Lord, hear my voice. Let your ears be attentive to my cry for mercy. If you, LORD, kept a record of sins, Lord, who could stand? But with you there is forgiveness, so that we can, with reverence, serve you. I wait for the LORD, my whole being waits, and in his word I put my hope. I wait for the Lord more than watchmen wait for the morning, more than watchmen wait for the morning. Israel, put your hope in the LORD, for with the LORD is unfailing love and with him is full redemption. He himself will redeem Israel from all their sins.

Consider This

I get to be one of the co-pastors for a beautiful little church in Chapel Hill, North Carolina. Each of our pastors embraces a bi-vocational ministry approach, meaning we hold other jobs beyond the church. This strategy empowers intentional incarnation in our community and focuses more funds on our mission.

In the early days of our church plant I worked as a substitute teacher in our local school system. Glamorous, I know. I imagined myself in a scene from *Dead Poets Society*, changing lives with my lectures on *To Kill a Mockingbird*, inspiring young minds to discover their dreams and follow their hero into the noble life of substitute teaching.

Instead, most of my instruction boiled down to me saying, "Under no circumstance is it ever appropriate to use that word to describe anyone or anything."

So, you can understand my surprise when I heard something that grabbed my attention in a good way. Once, in a class discussion about a short story, middle school students were describing the mood created by the author. One soft-spoken, shaggy-haired kid offered this assessment: "The story is tense, scary, and dangerous all the way through. But even though you feel afraid, hope is always present."

And there it is.

The student's description of that short story captures the thrust of the whole story, the cry of Psalm 130, the longing realized in Advent.

Advent is a season of robust hope. It is the kind of hope that is always present, not merely an idea planted firmly in the future. Jesus takes what is future, what is far off, and drags it into the present. He buries it in us like a seed, waiting for the harvest. We may not see the flourishing right now, but it is there, taking root and stretching out in the soil of our souls. Hope is present where we need it the most—in the thick of it, where the road closes in and the end seems cut off.

When it seems as if there is no hope, we remember that is precisely the one thing we do have. We light a wreath of candles as an act of defiance against the darkness.

We proclaim the anthem of Advent, the disruptive genius of "God with us." With us as we cry out from the depths. With us in our pain, our tragedy, our longing. With us to empower premeditated love, even in the face of fear. With us to form his people into a living protest against the way things are, and a prophetic vision of what should be and could be and one day will be.

He is with us as we wait for Advent all over again, watching and hoping for the return of our long-expected Jesus. Like a watchman waits for the morning.

The Prayer
Jesus, hope is always present because you are.

The Questions
- How do you see hope present with you today?
- How does hope change the way you see the present you are in?

AND THE WORD BECAME FLESH,
AND MADE HIS DWELLING AMONG US.

6 You Are Spoken For

RUTH 4:14–17 | The women said to Naomi: "Praise be to the LORD, who this day has not left you without a guardian-redeemer. May he become famous throughout Israel! He will renew your life and sustain you in your old age. For your daughter-in-law, who loves you and who is better to you than seven sons, has given him birth."

Then Naomi took the child in her arms and cared for him. The women living there said, "Naomi has a son!" And they named him Obed. He was the father of Jesse, the father of David.

Consider This

Several years ago we went to hear our friend John in concert, singing songs from his native Kenya. One song in particular made its mark on me. As he sang from somewhere down in the deepest part of his soul, the sound had this ancient timbre to it, while the spirit of his dance could only be characterized as freedom.

A single word came to mind as I watched him: *joy*. It was on his face, in his voice, all over his dance. When he translated the lyrics, I suddenly understood why. It was a traditional wedding song. The chorus said, "He is hers. She is his."

There is joy in knowing you are spoken for, joy in receiving love and giving it in return. It is this kind of joy that we find at work in the Old Testament story of Ruth.

Ruth was the daughter-in-law of Naomi. Having both lost their husbands, they were abandoned and alone. Two widows with nothing in the world but each other. Their situation was so desperate, Naomi (which can mean "beautiful") wanted to change her name to Mara (which means "bitter"). From beautiful to bitter. That was their storyline. And they were convinced that their story was over.

But in this sweeping mystery of redemption, the end is often an unexpected beginning. Or, as the poet T. S. Eliot in his poem "Little Gidding" put it, "The end is where we start from."

Ruth meets Boaz, an honorable relative whose story seemed stalled as well. Through a divinely directed turn of events, he takes Ruth as his wife. He spreads his protection and provision over her, and together they give birth to a son.

In the end, Ruth, Naomi, and Boaz all find a new beginning. Boaz becomes the great-grandfather of King David. Ruth, a foreigner, finds herself in the line of Israel's Messiah. And Naomi finds the beauty in life again. The Author takes our stalled stories and bends them toward his purpose and glory. Together they become a pivotal chapter in the Advent journey, their unexpected joy foreshadowing our own.

The story of Ruth is about much more than the marriage of this man and wife in ancient times. It is about the grand narrative of the gospel. God choosing you as his own. The joy in knowing that you are not abandoned, you are desired. You are not forgotten, you are redeemed.

You are spoken for. And your story is not over yet.

The Prayer

Author of our story, bend the arc to our good and your glory.

The Questions

- When has your story felt stalled, or even over?
- How was God's grace sufficient for you in that season?
- What did redemption look like?

AND THE WORD BECAME FLESH,
AND MADE HIS DWELLING AMONG US.

P. S. The story of Ruth is not about the search for a soul-mate or encouragement to those waiting for marriage to happen to them. Let's celebrate marriage for the gift that it is, but too often the church gets trapped in tired narratives about singleness as only a season and marriage as a sign of spiritual arrival. We need to honor the journey of those who choose the single life and embrace celibacy as a vow of holy surrender. If that describes you, and you've felt overlooked or marginalized by the church, then let me say I'm sorry. And please hear that your story matters. Not the story someone else sees for you. The story you are in right now.

7 The Singer

ZEPHANIAH 3:14–17 | Sing, Daughter Zion; shout aloud, Israel! Be glad and rejoice with all your heart, Daughter

Jerusalem! The Lord has taken away your punishment, he has turned back your enemy. The Lord, the King of Israel, is with you; never again will you fear any harm. On that day they will say to Jerusalem, "Do not fear, Zion; do not let your hands hang limp. The Lord your God is with you, the Mighty Warrior who saves. He will take great delight in you; in his love he will no longer rebuke you, but will rejoice over you with singing."

Consider This

Today, the world is filled with music. As Christ draws near, our joy takes the familiar shape of song and carol. What other season is so tied to melody? What other event in human history has sparked so much music? And for good reason. The anticipation of the arrival of Jesus at Christmas gives us something worth singing about.

It's always been this way. The first two chapters of the Gospel of Luke read like a hymnal, recording the responses of Zechariah at the birth of John the Baptist, the Magnificat of Mary when she learns of Jesus' coming, and the chorus of the angels filling the skies with brilliance and glory.

Why songs? They are not essential. They are not very practical. There are far more efficient and clear ways to communicate an idea. Songs are not essential, but instead they are extravagant. The overflow of the excess of the heart. They are a means of expressing the heart when mere words won't do the trick.

Songs are an offered-up act of beauty. And what better way for us to respond to the act of beauty offered up in

Christmas? They orient us again in truth that can't be neatly contained within lists of pro and con, ledgers of black and red. Zephaniah charges us in this passage to sing and shout and rejoice, even in the face of fear. To raise our voices against the chaos that we face, not in anger, but with a song. As the farmer-poet Wendell Berry in his poem "Manifesto: The Mad Farmer Liberation Front" put it, "So, friends, every day do something that won't compute. . . . Be joyful though you have considered all the facts." Why? Because the one who defends us also delights over us. The songs we sing don't start with us. They are echoes back to the Singer himself. Zephaniah tells us that our Mighty Warrior God is singing over us. What a strange thought. Yes, we sing to him from the overflow of our joy. But imagine a God so filled with love for his people that he sings to us from the overflow of his joy.

When there's nothing you can say to capture the power of a moment, sometimes you have to let lyrics speak for you. Sometimes you have to let the melody translate what is happening in your heart. Sometimes all you can do is sing.

The Prayer

Holy Spirit, sing the truth and strength and grace over us and teach us to live in step with your music.

The Questions

- What song captures the reality of where you are in life right now?

- What do you think the Singer is singing over you today?
- How can you join his song?

> AND THE WORD BECAME FLESH,
> AND MADE HIS DWELLING AMONG US.

Blessed Is the Peacemaker

8

ISAIAH 2:1–5 | This is what Isaiah son of Amoz saw concerning Judah and Jerusalem: In the last days the mountain of the Lord's temple will be established as the highest of the mountains; it will be exalted above the hills, and all nations will stream to it. Many peoples will come and say, "Come, let us go up to the mountain of the Lord, to the temple of the God of Jacob. He will teach us his ways, so that we may walk in his paths." The law will go out from Zion, the word of the Lord from Jerusalem. He will judge between the nations and will settle disputes for many peoples. They will beat their swords into plowshares and their spears into pruning hooks. Nation will not take up sword against nation, nor will they train for war anymore.

Come, descendants of Jacob, let us walk in the light of the Lord.

Consider This

"Come, let us go up to the mountain of the Lord." Isaiah's invitation to ascend the mountain is an invitation to experience

the presence of God. Throughout the Scripture narrative, the mountain is symbolic of the meeting place with God. Moses and Elijah, pillars of the Law and Prophets, both have mountaintop encounters where the Divine Glory is revealed. But in the miracle of the incarnation, the mountain of the Lord has come down to us. The Presence himself has made his dwelling among us, not descending in fire and cloud but in flesh and blood.

And the arrival of his presence will bring the arrival of peace. Blessed is the peacemaker, Isaiah encourages us, for he will embrace enemies and call them the children of God. He sees a coming revolution, where weapons of destruction will become tools of cultivation, from equipment designed to take lives to equipment designed to sustain and nurture life. Warriors transformed into farmers. What is hidden here is that this is a reversal of what was a common scene in the ancient world. When your home or village or nation was attacked, everyone became a warrior and everyday tools formed a makeshift arsenal. When war came to your land, the farmers became fighters, reaching for every blade and sharp edge to be used as sword or spear to defend their tribes and homes. But Isaiah foresees that when this Prince of Peace arrives among us, warriors are reversed into farmers and swords into plows. When his conquest rolls in, perfect love drives out fear and battle morphs into healing.

This is a grand vision of an ultimate and final peace. But the healing and peace starts in the immediate, here and now, first with God and then with others, all by Christ. And how far will that peace spread? To the most difficult places of all. Not only in an abstract, universal sense, but into our own broken relationships, families, and homes which often feel like the most war-torn of territories.

It's interesting that this passage from Isaiah builds to this invitation: "Come, descendants of Jacob, let us walk in the light of the LORD." The name *Jacob* alone reminds us of a broken family history, not only enemies across boundary lines, but within blood lines. Retrace the line and remember that Jacob's story begins with Abraham, the father of Isaac and Ishmael, two brothers who become enemies. Isaac has twin sons, Esau and Jacob, who become enemies. Jacob has twelve sons, with eleven turning against Joseph in betrayal. These twelve sons become the twelve tribes of Israel, who will later divide into two separate kingdoms. Jesus even tells his most memorable story by beginning with the words, "There once was a [father] who had two sons . . ." (Matt. 21:28).

Out of their division God brings peace to the world, and through Jesus the Father shows that he desires to restore the Isaacs and Ishmaels to each other and himself. From the time of Cain and Abel, sin has been turning family into enemies. But the Prince of Peace has come to turn enemies into family.

The Prayer

Peacemaker, bring your reign of peace to our broken places.

The Questions
- What relationships need healing in the here and now?
- How can you become a peacemaker in that place?

> AND THE WORD BECAME FLESH,
> AND MADE HIS DWELLING AMONG US.

9 Joy to the World (Or, How to Write a Better Song)

PHILIPPIANS 2:6–11 (NIV 1984) | Who, being in very nature God, did not consider equality with God as something to be grasped; rather, he made himself nothing by taking the very nature of a servant, being made in human likeness. And being found in appearance as a man, he humbled himself by becoming obedient to death—even death on a cross! Therefore God exalted him to the highest place and gave him the name that is above every name, that at the name of Jesus every knee should bow, in heaven and on earth and under the earth, and every tongue acknowledge that Jesus Christ is Lord, to the glory of God the Father.

Consider This

One of the first songs of this season is the anthem, "Joy to the World." Originally intended to be a song about the second coming of Jesus, subsequent generations adopted it as the theme song of his first coming at Christmas. This classic was penned by the prolific hymn writer Isaac Watts, one of more than seven hundred works created by Watts in worship of Jesus. When he was a young man, he frequently complained about the music he was experiencing in church. He called it boring, hard to sing, and lacking true heart-level zeal. Finally, his father challenged him to stop complaining and do something about it. If you don't like it, change it. Write a better song.

And, indeed, he did. Seven hundred times over.

While "Joy to the World" is one of the first songs of this season, scholars believe that today's passage from Paul's letter to the Philippians is one of the first songs of the church. It is quoted in this letter as if it is a hymn or poem familiar to the hearers, an early form of liturgy expressing worship of the Word made flesh. Notice the pattern carved out in the lines. They begin with Jesus in the highest possible place, naming him as being in very nature God. Then, he steps into our story, making his descent into flesh and cross and grave. Then the grand pivot as he is raised up once again in resurrection and exalted glory above all things. This is the Great Reversal of humanity's story. On the one hand, we knew harmony with God in the garden, but that wasn't enough. We grasped after equality with him. Jesus, on the other hand, "being in very nature God, did not consider equality with God as something to be grasped." We were convinced to make something of ourselves. Jesus made himself nothing. While our sin follows a trajectory of fall and brokenness and death, his death pioneers resurrection and healing and life.

In the garden, sin silenced the melody. In Advent, Jesus writes a better song.

And we get swept up in it. We hear the Lord himself rejoicing and singing over us, and we start to pick up the melody again, learning the rhythm, feeling out our part. We join the better song and sing out the anthem of the first Advent and the Advent yet to come, "Joy to world! The Lord is come. Let earth receive her King."[2]

The Prayer

Name above every name, we bow our knee and acknowledge that Jesus Christ is Lord, to the glory of God the Father.

The Questions

- What changes do you long to see in the world?
- How can you embody that change and write a better song?
- How is the Holy Spirit transforming you in the pattern of Christ as described in today's passage?

AND THE WORD BECAME FLESH,
AND MADE HIS DWELLING AMONG US.

---

2. Isaac Watts, "Joy to the World! the Lord Is Come!" 1719, public domain.

Love Local (Go Small and Go Home)

10

COLOSSIANS 1:15–20 | The Son is the image of the invisible God, the firstborn over all creation. For in him all things were created: things in heaven and on earth, visible and invisible, whether thrones or powers or rulers or authorities; all things have been created through him and for him. He is before all things, and in him all things hold together. And he is the head of the body, the church; he is the beginning and the firstborn from among the dead, so that in everything he might have the supremacy. For God was pleased to have all his fullness dwell in him, and through him to reconcile to himself all things, whether things on earth or things in heaven, by making peace through his blood, shed on the cross.

Consider This

It was one of those mornings. My twin sons, Luke and Sam, were about five or six years old. And they once again transformed the drive to school into an open forum question-and-answer session where no theological curiosity was off-limits. I did my best to answer in a way they could grasp. It went something like this:

Luke: Dad, if Jesus is in my heart, how can he be in heaven at the same time?

Me: Great question, buddy. Because Jesus is God and he can be everywhere at once.

Luke: But, Dad, I thought there was only one Jesus. How can one person be everywhere?

Me: Another great question. He is so big that he fills up everything, everywhere so he can be everywhere and right there with you at the same time.

Sam: But, Dad, if Jesus is so big, then why can't we see him?

These kindergarten/kingdom-sized curiosities are answered in Advent. This season of mystery invites and awakens childlike faith. Not just to grasp the right answers. But to keep asking the right questions.

Author Madeleine L'Engle employed the phrase "the irrational season" to describe this journey we're on. This moment that asks us to believe the impossible and stake everything on it. That the massive God who fills all things makes himself small enough to see. For all the times he reveals himself through fire and flood and plague and blinding glory, in this moment we see him most clearly. As the Transcendent descends, the Universal localized—the image of the invisible God.

In addition to my role as theology student under Luke and Sam, I'm also one of the pastors at a quirky little church called Love Chapel Hill in downtown Chapel Hill, North Carolina. Our name is our mission: love Chapel Hill with the heart of Jesus. In the early days of planting this church, we often heard hyped-up strategists and leadership experts repeat the rallying cry, "go big or go home." Instead, we took on the counter approach of "go small and go home." In other words, start small, right where we are. Love local, we like to say, as a reminder that the next opportunity to proclaim the gospel of Jesus is not waiting in the spotlight on the biggest stage, but right in front of us as we walk down the street, hiding in the form of outcast or neighbor or stranger. Every moment is an opportunity to make the highest truth and deepest theology and largest love small enough to see.

Of course, this is no innovation. It is simply an imitation of the image of the invisible God. The one in whom all the fullness of God dwells, and yet he comes and dwells with us. The massive God who fills all things and makes himself small enough to see.

The Prayer

God of fullness who fills all things, make yourself small enough to see through me. And give me eyes to see you made small through others.

The Questions

- How can you love local, or go small and go home?
- What is one small way you can help one person to see the love of Jesus in you?

> AND THE WORD BECAME FLESH,
> AND MADE HIS DWELLING AMONG US.

11 | Don't Forget the Fire

MALACHI 3:1–4 | "I will send my messenger, who will prepare the way before me. Then suddenly the Lord you are seeking will come to his temple; the messenger of the covenant, whom you desire, will come," says the LORD Almighty.

But who can endure the day of his coming? Who can stand when he appears? For he will be like a refiner's fire or a launderer's soap. He will sit as a refiner and purifier of silver; he will purify the Levites and refine them like gold and silver. Then the LORD will have men who will bring offerings in righteousness, and the offerings of Judah and Jerusalem will be acceptable to the LORD, as in days gone by, as in former years.

Consider This

Malachi is the last of the minor prophets, the final book of the Old Testament. His name means, "My Messenger," which is fitting since the thrust of his book is the promise that God is sending his messenger to us. One last promise of Advent—that God has not forgotten or abandoned us—but in the silence, he is scripting our salvation and rescue.

The promise of this messenger brings us much joy and hope and peace. But it should also make us highly uncomfortable. Because Malachi employs imagery in this passage that we don't often associate with Advent. The prophet warns that the Light of the World is a fire. Not just the warm glow of an Advent candle or the soft gleam of a distant star. A blazing fire. We rejoice as Malachi declares, "the messenger of the covenant, whom you desire, will come." But we begin to tremble when Malachi asks, "But who can endure the day of his coming? Who can stand when he appears?"

We understand the threat of fire. It has the power to bring destruction when it is unleashed. In Scripture, it's often tied to the idea of God's righteous judgment.

But fire can also be harnessed to bring about transformation and purification. Perhaps this is why fire is also tied to the idea of God's intense presence in Scripture. He is a refiner's fire who draws close, bent on purifying and transforming us into priceless gold. In Jesus, he takes the judgment upon himself. He endures the fall so that we can stand in the day of his coming. This is holy love! The brilliance and blaze of this refiner's fire does not destroy us. It transforms us.

When we think of this season, we often reflect on what Jesus brings. But Malachi reminds us he has also come to take away. To give his life and take away our sin. To give his holiness and take away our brokenness. To burn away all that is not gold and cannot survive the refinement process. So what is he taking away in you? What in your life will not survive the flames of holy love?

We know that the world is desperate for change. And we believe that Jesus is the one who can change it. But perhaps he wants to begin right there with you. And he will not quit. He loves you too much to do anything less than take you all the way.

Our view of his arrival can be sentimental. And it's okay to bask in the glow of the season and its heartwarming traditions. But don't forget the fire. This baby in the manger has come to shatter your categories and upend your expectations and transform your life. So let your heart be filled with hope, experience the joy and wonder, soak in the peace. But brace yourself. He has come to change the world. And you along with it.

The Prayer

Refiner's Fire, I surrender to your flames. Transform me through your holy love.

The Questions

- What is the Refiner's fire burning away in you?
- What is not gold and needs to go?

AND THE WORD BECAME FLESH,
AND MADE HIS DWELLING AMONG US.

12 Broken Branches

MATTHEW 1:1 | This is the genealogy of Jesus the Messiah the son of David, the son of Abraham: . . .

Consider This

Matthew begins his gospel with the genealogy of Jesus, tracing the roots of his family tree. To the modern reader, this seems like a terrible way to start a story. Our eyes glaze over and minds wander as he recites branch after branch of names that mean nothing to us. But Matthew is not only establishing that Jesus was born into the unbroken royal line of David, but that he was also born into the broken storyline of humanity.

The names Abraham and David stir up memory of God's covenant with his people. His faithfulness to them fuels our hope in Advent as we await the ultimate child of promise, that brightest star in Abraham's sky, who will reign on David's throne as our anointed Shepherd King. And yet these names cast a shadow as well, their failures sowing the seeds of ancestral sin.

Matthew makes a strange move in recounting the history of Jesus' arrival. Against the tradition of his patriarchal society and time, he chooses to include the names of women in this lineage. And not just any names. There is Tamar, a victim of injustice who in turn disguises herself as a prostitute in order to deceive her father-in-law, Judah. She becomes pregnant by him and their offspring becomes an ancestor of the Messiah. Then there is Rahab, a prostitute by trade who rescues the spies of Joshua in Jericho. She plays a key role in that military victory and eventually takes her place in the family line of the Savior. And Ruth, a foreigner from enemy territory who marries Rahab's son and becomes the great-grandmother of King David.

And speaking of David, Matthew lists him here alongside Bathsheba. David drags her into this genealogy by way of lust, adultery, betrayal, and murder. (Try to make a Christmas card out of that.) He sleeps with Bathsheba while her husband Uriah is fighting David's war. After she conceives, he arranges for Uriah to be abandoned in battle, killing him to cover the sin.

Now, a word for Bathsheba. She is often cast as a temptress who seduces David and draws him into her web. But please remember the story. This takes place in a patriarchal society where David, military hero and man after God's own heart, serves as a monarch divinely chosen by God himself. All of the power rests on David in this scenario. We should not see this as a passionate affair. Instead, this is a tragic abuse of power. And God will not stand for it. David is confronted and judged. And God refuses to reject Bathsheba, bringing her into the line of Jesus.

Matthew shows us that Jesus came through a lineage of broken people to heal and save and redeem broken people. He is like the artist that salvages unexpected materials and breathes beauty into them. From the broken pieces of our story, he carefully constructs a stunning mosaic of grace that shouts forgiveness is possible and redemption is coming for you.

The journey from Sarah's womb to Mary's is marked with willing sin, gut-wrenching injustice, and the grotesque abuse of power. Those who sin and are sinned against. It's into the middle of this reality—our reality—that Jesus is born, reversing the trajectory of the entire story. He confronts us with the truth that sin is strong, but grace is stronger. Sin doesn't get the final say. Because of a little baby born in Bethlehem, grace always has the last word.

Remember this: You aren't the only one with a past; God has one too. Peace is knowing that your past is not nearly as defining as his.

The Prayer
God of the past, present, and future, I surrender the broken pieces to you.

The Questions
- What parts of your past need to be healed?
- How might God bend even that toward redemption?

AND THE WORD BECAME FLESH,
AND MADE HIS DWELLING AMONG US.

Clay Pots, Trumpets, and a Child Is Born

13

ISAIAH 9:1–7 | Nevertheless, there will be no more gloom for those who were in distress. In the past he humbled the land of Zebulun and the land of Naphtali, but in the future he will honor Galilee of the nations, by the Way of the Sea, beyond the Jordan—

The people walking in darkness have seen a great light; on those living in the land of deep darkness a light has dawned. You have enlarged the nation and increased their joy; they rejoice before you as people rejoice at the harvest, as warriors rejoice when dividing the plunder. For as in the day of Midian's defeat, you have shattered the yoke that burdens them, the bar across their shoulders, the rod of their oppressor. Every warrior's boot used in battle and every garment rolled in blood will be destined for burning, will be fuel for the fire. For to us a child is born, to us a son is given, and the government will be on his shoulders. And he will be called Wonderful Counselor, Mighty God, Everlasting Father, Prince of Peace. Of the greatness of his government and peace there will be no end. He will reign on David's throne and over his kingdom, establishing and upholding it with justice and righteousness from that time on and forever. The zeal of the LORD Almighty will accomplish this.

Consider This

This is one of the signature passages of Advent. It's vintage Isaiah, a poetic vision of the hope realized in the arrival of Jesus. We return to it year after year. We read and sing and preach the familiar themes about Galilee and the great light and the government on his shoulders. And Handel's *Messiah* starts to play in our heads on loop. It just happened to you right now, didn't it?

But in the midst of this passage is a reference in verse 4 to a person we don't often associate with the season. He gets no shout-out in our carols, no mention in our Christmas cards, no bathrobe cameo in our Nativity plays. But Isaiah says that the arrival of our rescue will be like another Gideon moment.

He compares the coming of our Savior to what he calls "the day of Midian's defeat."

This line refers back to Judges 6 and 7 when Israel was being oppressed by their enemy Midian. Though their sin and rebellion invited this judgment, God in his unrelenting mercy raised up yet another rescue for his people. Once again, he selects an unlikely leader armed with an unexpected instrument to carry out his unconventional strategy.

Gideon reduces his army to a mere three hundred men and camps outside of the Midian stronghold. At the Lord's direction, they enact a ridiculous battle plan, consisting of smashing clay pots, blowing trumpets, and holding up torches. Against all odds, the inspired plan actually works. The mighty army of Midian is thrown into confusion and fear, turning on each other in the chaos and destroying itself before Gideon's army raises a sword or draws an arrow.

Isaiah tells us that Advent is like that. The arrival of our rescue in Jesus is an echo of what God did for Israel through Gideon. But as in the day of Midian's defeat, we are shocked when we consider the strategy he employs to break our oppression and overthrow the threat against us. We lean in to hear the battle plan, the tactical genius of our Mighty Warrior. And equipped with the strength of angel armies, he goes with this: "For to us a child is born, to us a son is given."

We rejoice as Israel did because, like them, we have known the night. We have felt the weight of the yoke, splintered by the bar, broken by the rod. We rejoice because the strong one has come to shatter them. We have been crushed by the warrior's boot. That is our blood on their garments. So we rejoice when we see them go up in flames.

But our rejoicing is only matched by our wonder. We've been watching for our rescue. But we never saw this coming. Wilder than clay pots and torches, we get a virgin singing a lullaby over a manger. A baby cries in the night and hell trembles at the sound. For as in the days of Midian's defeat . . . it's a story only he could write.

The Prayer

God of angel armies, give me eyes to see you moving in ways I could never expect.

The Questions

- What unconventional strategy is Jesus employing in your life right now?
- What Gideon moment do you need? Where are you over-matched and underequipped and in desperate need of his help? Have you asked him for it?
- Bonus question: Who is going to write the first Advent hymn featuring Gideon?

AND THE WORD BECAME FLESH,
AND MADE HIS DWELLING AMONG US.

A Borrowed Song

14

LUKE 2:13–15 | Suddenly a great company of the heavenly host appeared with the angel, praising God and saying,

"Glory to God in the highest heaven, and on earth peace to those on whom his favor rests."

When the angels had left them and gone into heaven, the shepherds said to one another, "Let's go to Bethlehem and see this thing that has happened, which the Lord has told us about."

Consider This

I heard the bells on Christmas Day
Their old, familiar carols play,
And wild and sweet
The words repeat
Of peace on earth, good-will to men!

This classic Christmas carol was written by the renowned American poet Henry Wadsworth Longfellow. And as the lyrics suggest, he crafted it after hearing the local church bells ringing in the celebration of Christmas Day.

But here's the thing. He wrote this on Christmas Day 1863.

In the throes of the American Civil War.

Our nation was being torn apart and swallowed by turmoil. The violence and bloodshed were unthinkable. Too many fathers and sons were missing from the family table that day. Many never to return.

Longfellow's own son was badly wounded while fighting for the Union, and his survival was still in question. Which is why he answers the first verse with another.

And in despair, I bowed my head
"There is no peace on earth," I said;
"For hate is strong
And mocks the song
Of peace on earth, good-will to men!"

These words seem more like reality. And as they spoke to the turmoil and chaos of those days, they ring true in our time as well.

But Christians are strange people. In the midst of tragedy, we often find ourselves reaching for a song. Not in naive denial. But as an act of defiance. A protest against the way things are. A prophetic and poetic vision of how they could be, should be, will be. Advent teaches us to sing in the dark. With the stubborn hope that the Light is on the way.

And that's exactly why our poet friend writes yet another verse. We will give the last word to Mr. Longfellow and borrow his song for the season we find ourselves in.

Then pealed the bells more loud and deep:
"God is not dead, nor doth He sleep;
The Wrong shall fail,
The Right prevail,
With peace on earth, good-will to men"

The Prayer

God of Peace, prevail in the thick of our chaos. God of Light, teach us to sing in the dark.

The Questions

- Which verse of this song do you relate to the most?
- How is heaven singing a defiant peace into your life?

AND THE WORD BECAME FLESH,
AND MADE HIS DWELLING AMONG US.

Yahweh Remembers 15

LUKE 1:5–17 | In the time of Herod king of Judea there was a priest named Zechariah, who belonged to the priestly division of Abijah; his wife Elizabeth was also a descendant of Aaron. Both of them were righteous in the sight of God, observing all the Lord's commands and decrees blamelessly. But they were childless because Elizabeth was not able to conceive, and they were both very old.

Once when Zechariah's division was on duty and he was serving as priest before God, he was chosen by lot, according to the custom of the priesthood, to go into the temple of the Lord and burn incense. And when the time for the burning of incense came, all the assembled worshipers were praying outside.

Then an angel of the Lord appeared to him, standing at the right side of the altar of incense. When Zechariah saw him, he was startled and was gripped with fear. But the angel said to him: "Do not be afraid, Zechariah; your prayer has been heard. Your wife Elizabeth will bear you a son, and you are to call him John. He will be a joy and delight to you, and many will rejoice because of his birth, for he will be great in the sight of the Lord. He is never to take wine or other fermented drink, and he will be filled with the Holy Spirit even before he is born. He will bring back many of the people of Israel to the Lord their God. And he will go on before the Lord, in the spirit and power of Elijah, to turn the hearts of the parents to their children and the disobedient to the wisdom of the righteous—to make ready a people prepared for the Lord."

Consider This

Luke begins this narrative by establishing the setting within its historical context. He tells us that these events take place "In the time Herod king of Judea." But before we even finish the paragraph, we learn that this opening sentence has been made obsolete. For all of Herod's political maneuvering, collecting of power, building monuments to himself, solidifying his place among the great leaders of history, this will no longer be known as the time of Herod. We are nearing the arrival of King Jesus and, from this point on, time itself will be marked by his birth. Herod is about to be overshadowed by the Light himself.

How is God wanting to redefine the time you find yourself in? You've named this the time of your unemployment or your divorce. The time of undergrad, grad school, doctoral work. The time of waiting, sickness, addiction, depression, uncertainty. I wonder what story the Author is telling that will redefine the time you're in?

As Luke introduces the story of Zechariah and Elizabeth, we find a microcosm of the larger story of Israel, and truly, all of creation. Theirs is a story marked by waiting and hoping. For years they longed to have children, but had come to terms with the harsh reality that their eyes would never see the fulfillment of this hope and their hearts would never experience the joy of this longing. Exiled in the desert of waiting, they thought they would never see the promise. Their hopes waned in the stifling silence of God.

Perhaps you've been there? You've known what the desert feels like. How do you respond to God when it feels like he is not responding to you?

Despite his disappointment, we find Zechariah in worship. He hasn't let his heartbreak become bitterness against God. Instead, he is leaning into him. Not as an escape to forget the pain of reality. But as an engagement with the ultimate reality. Worship is reality, a declaration of the most real reality that Yahweh is God and I am his.

In this moment, an angel appears to him with this proclamation, "Do not be afraid, Zechariah; your prayer has been heard." This is the great promise of Advent. Do not be afraid! Your prayer has been heard! We were in desperate need for a Savior. And God heard our prayer. And we marvel at the kindness of God. As he moves to answer the deepest longing of creation on a cosmic scale, he begins by fulfilling the hope of one couple, convinced they had been forgotten. A hidden beauty is that Zechariah's name means "Yahweh remembers." For his entire life, every time he heard someone call his name, every time he introduced himself, seeds of promise were being planted in his soul. And those seeds burst into harvest when he heard his name from the mouth of Gabriel. "Do not be afraid, Zechariah; your prayer has been heard." You have not been forgotten. Yahweh remembers.

Zechariah and Elizabeth will become parents of John the Baptist, the trailblazer for Jesus the Messiah. And the redemption of their pain is the beginning of our healing.

The Prayer

God who hears and remembers, help me to trust that you hear and remember me.

The Questions

- What prayer remains unanswered in your life or what longing is yet unfulfilled?
- What need, what fear, what obstacle threatens you?
- How might the redemption of your pain be the beginning of someone else's healing?

AND THE WORD BECAME FLESH,
AND MADE HIS DWELLING AMONG US.

Daddy King

16

LUKE 1:26–33 | In the sixth month of Elizabeth's pregnancy, God sent the angel Gabriel to Nazareth, a town in Galilee, to a virgin pledged to be married to a man named Joseph, a descendant of David. The virgin's name was Mary. The angel went to her and said, "Greetings, you who are highly favored! The Lord is with you."

Mary was greatly troubled at his words and wondered what kind of greeting this might be. But the angel said to her, "Do not be afraid, Mary; you have found favor with God. You will conceive and give birth to a son, and you are to call him Jesus. He will be great and will be called the Son of the Most High. The Lord God will give him the throne of his father David, and he will reign over Jacob's descendants forever; his kingdom will never end."

Consider This

One of my heroes has long been Dr. Martin Luther King Jr.

Yet it pains me to confess that I knew next to nothing about his father, Dr. Martin Luther King Sr. "Daddy King," as he was affectionately known within his family and throughout the civil rights movement, was the pastor of Ebenezer Baptist Church in Atlanta, Georgia. The younger King was actually an associate pastor, serving under the leadership of his father.

Daddy King suffered unthinkable tragedy in his life. The nation joined his mourning over the brutal assassination of

Martin Jr., but he lost his youngest son, Alfred, as well, only one year later in a mysterious drowning. Alfred had been on his college swim team, which led many to suspect foul play in his death. And shortly after that, he even lost his beloved wife. A gunman entered their church and shot Mrs. Alberta King while she sat playing the organ.

So much heartache. How does one person bear such pain? And yet, the witnesses remember that through the rest of his ministry, Daddy King never stopped preaching the gospel of Jesus' radical love. A love that extends even to those who hate you and hurt you. A love that forgives murderers and reimagines enemies as candidates for grace.

Suddenly, the legacy and courage of the younger Dr. King makes sense. In the son, we are seeing what the father is like.

Scripture gives many names to Jesus. Isaiah calls him the Wonderful Counselor, Prince of Peace, Immanuel. Malachi calls him the Refiner's Fire and Messenger of the Covenant. Jeremiah sees him as the Righteous Branch of David's line. But in Luke 2, the angel Gabriel says we will call him the Son of the Most High God.

Because he is the Most High God, he is utterly above and beyond us in every way—holiness ablaze and untouchable. How could we ever know him? Through the Son. Paul claims that Jesus is the image of the invisible God. In other words, in the Son, we are seeing what the Father is like.

The revered missionary to India, E. Stanley Jones, put it this way:

If God thinks in terms of little children as Jesus did, cares for the leper, the outcast, and the blind, and if his heart is like that gentle heart that broke upon the cross, then he can have my heart without reservation and without question. . . . The greatest news that has ever been broken to the human race is the news that God is like Christ. And the greatest news we can break to that non-Christian world is just that—that the God whom you have dimly realized, but about whose character you are uncertain, is like Christ.[3]

Jones said it right. The grand news from Gabriel is that our salvation will be called the Son of the Most High God. And in this Son we will see what the Father is like.

The Prayer
Son of the Most High God, show us what the Father is like. And by your grace, make us like him too.

The Questions
- Is the transforming power of the Son evident in your life?
- When people look at you, can they see him?

AND THE WORD BECAME FLESH,
AND MADE HIS DWELLING AMONG US.

---

3. E. Stanley Jones, *The Christ of the Indian Road* (Nashville, TN: Abingdon Press, 1925), 49.

17 Look Again

JOHN 1:9–13 | The true light that gives light to everyone was coming into the world. He was in the world, and though the world was made through him, the world did not recognize him. He came to that which was his own, but his own did not receive him. Yet to all who did receive him, to those who believed in his name, he gave the right to become children of God—children born not of natural descent, nor of human decision or a husband's will, but born of God.

Consider This

Several years ago, *Washington Post* columnist Gene Weingarten conducted what he called "an experiment in . . . perception." He set out to answer the question, "In a banal setting at an inconvenient time, would beauty transcend?"[4]

He enlisted the help of world-renowned violin virtuoso Joshua Bell, convincing him to play in a bustling Washington DC metro station during rush hour. Now, here's something you need to know: Bell plays a handcrafted 1713 Stradivarius violin, reportedly worth $3.5 million. Just days before, he sold out Boston Symphony Hall, where many of the tickets went

---

4. Gene Weingarten, "Pearls Before Breakfast: Can one of the nation's greatest musicians cut through the fog of D.C. rush hour? Let's find out," *Washington Post* (April 8, 2007), https://www.washingtonpost.com/lifestyle/magazine/pearls-before-breakfast-can-one-of-the-nations-great-musicians-cut-through-the-fog-of-a-dc-rush-hour-lets-find-out/2014/09/23/8a6d46da-4331-11e4-b47c-f5889e061e5f_story.html?utm_term=.a86a7e9a84f4.

for one hundred dollars a piece (because you have to pay for that violin somehow).

So there he was, treasured talent, playing his treasured instrument, like a common street performer. Would anyone notice? Would they perceive?

In the forty-five minutes that he played that day, with more than a thousand passengers passing by, twenty-seven people paused just long enough to drop a little change in his hat. (Totaling $32.17. You're not paying for the violin like that.) Seven people stopped for any length of time to take in the beauty of the moment. One person recognized who he was. In the routine of the everyday, in the rush of the moment, almost everyone failed to perceive.

Advent is an invitation to perceive. Christmas calls us to look again.

We are drawing close to the culmination of this journey from darkness to light. And as the waiting and anticipation moves toward fulfillment, this is a moment to pause. This is a moment to confront John's harsh assessment that those who waited for the Messiah failed to see him. This is a moment to look again.

Look again at the story you've seen repeated every single year of your life and pause long enough to find it fresh.

Look again at Joseph. His reputation trashed in honor of the woman he loves and the God he serves. He will raise the one who will raise the dead. He will teach the Creator how to be a carpenter. He will show God what it means to be a man.

Look again at Mary. From the first moments she has been in uncharted waters, and things won't get any easier from here. Time moves too quickly for any mom. Even more when your baby is born for a mission like this. But for now she will ponder it all in her heart and cherish every moment.

Look again at the baby. Look close. Take him in. This is our redemption. This is our seed of hope pushing up through the dirt after a bleak and bitter winter. This is beauty arriving at an inconvenient time and in an unexpected setting as the masses rush by.

This is an invitation to perceive. Christmas calls us to look again. What will you see?

A reminder: We not only look again; we look ahead. Advent is a season when we anticipate the arrival of Christ at Christmas. But it is also a season that calls us to watch for his second arrival, when the true Light that gives light to everyone will shatter the darkness and make all things new. May we have eyes to see.

The Prayer

Light of the world, help me to see you and to see the world around me in light of you.

The Questions

- Have you paused long enough to perceive this Advent season?

- How have you seen Jesus show up at inconvenient times and in unexpected places?
- Where will you see him today?

AND THE WORD BECAME FLESH,
AND MADE HIS DWELLING AMONG US.

The Way

18

ISAIAH 35:1–10 | The desert and the parched land will be glad; the wilderness will rejoice and blossom. Like the crocus, it will burst into bloom; it will rejoice greatly and shout for joy. The glory of Lebanon will be given to it, the splendor of Carmel and Sharon; they will see the glory of the Lord, the splendor of our God.

Strengthen the feeble hands, steady the knees that give way; say to those with fearful hearts, "Be strong, do not fear; your God will come, he will come with vengeance; with divine retribution he will come to save you."

Then will the eyes of the blind be opened and the ears of the deaf unstopped. Then will the lame leap like a deer, and the mute tongue shout for joy. Water will gush forth in the wilderness and streams in the desert. The burning sand will become a pool, the thirsty ground bubbling springs. In the haunts where jackals once lay, grass and reeds and papyrus will grow.

And a highway will be there; it will be called the Way of Holiness; it will be for those who walk on that Way. The unclean will not journey on it; wicked fools will not go about on it. No lion will be there, nor any ravenous beast; they will not be found there. But only the redeemed will walk there, and those the LORD has rescued will return. They will enter Zion with singing; everlasting joy will crown their heads. Gladness and joy will overtake them, and sorrow and sighing will flee away.

Consider This

The journey of Advent leads out of the desert and back to the garden. It's a movement from trial to rest, from preparation to fulfillment, from waiting to arrival, from searching to finding. Even better than finding, to be being found.

Isaiah 35 sparks our biblical imagination, calling to mind memories of the exodus and the journey through the desert. After generations of slavery in Egypt, God hears the cries of his people and does something about it. He raises up Moses to bring the mightiest empire on earth to its knees. He breaks the chains of oppression and delivers the people from their bondage.

At the same time, this passage looks forward to the ministry of John of Baptist, the trailblazing voice in the wilderness, preparing the way for another exodus. Isaiah's vision holds these two stories together, showing us that the Messiah who is coming will be our Moses, leading us out of slavery to sin and into the promise.

When John the pioneer is thrown into prison and begins to wonder if Jesus really is the Way, Jesus points him back to this very chapter in Isaiah. He sends this message to John: the blind see, the deaf hear, the lame leap, the stilled tongue shouts for joy. The wilderness through which you blazed a trail is springing to life. The desert is becoming a garden again.

Jesus is *the* Way we've been waiting for. But not a static gate or hidden passage that we must search for until we discover it. No. This Way is on the move. It winds through the farthest and forgotten corners of creation. It runs through the worst neighborhoods where others are afraid to go. It crosses lines and climbs walls. And finds us in the dry desert to lead us back home to freedom.

Jesus is most certainly the Way. And no one comes to the Father except through him. But the Father proves in the Advent moment that there is no place he is not willing to send Jesus to find us. Jesus carries with him all the hope of the kingdom, and when he catches you, joy and gladness will overtake you. In Advent, the Father catches us. And we cannot contain the pure joy of it. Like John the Baptist in his mother's womb, our hearts leap inside us as we hear the story, our dry deserts burst with life as the Life draws near. The Way himself searches us out and redirects our hearts back home again.

In Advent we don't find the way.

The Way finds us.

The Prayer

Jesus, find us where we are and bring the dead places to life.

The Questions
- Where are you in the journey? A desert or a garden, or some landscape in between?
- What dry places are choking the life out of you?
- How is he bringing the dead places to life?

AND THE WORD BECAME FLESH,
AND MADE HIS DWELLING AMONG US.

19 Remembering the Future

ISAIAH 11:1–9 | A shoot will come up from the stump of Jesse; from his roots a Branch will bear fruit. The Spirit of the LORD will rest on him—the Spirit of wisdom and of understanding, the Spirit of counsel and of might, the Spirit of the knowledge and fear of the LORD—and he will delight in the fear of the LORD.

He will not judge by what he sees with his eyes, or decide by what he hears with his ears; but with righteousness he will judge the needy, with justice he will give decisions for the poor of the earth. He will strike the earth with the rod of his mouth;

with the breath of his lips he will slay the wicked. Righteousness will be his belt and faithfulness the sash around his waist.

The wolf will live with the lamb, the leopard will lie down with the goat, the calf and the lion and the yearling together; and a little child will lead them. The cow will feed with the bear, their young will lie down together, and the lion will eat straw like the ox. The infant will play near the cobra's den, and the young child will put its hand into the viper's nest. They will neither harm nor destroy on all my holy mountain, for the earth will be filled with the knowledge of the LORD as the waters cover the sea.

Consider This

Isaiah leads into today's passage with an image of destruction. In the previous chapter he sees a once mighty forest reduced to a wasteland. He says even a child could count the trees and write them down. It's a glimpse of what has and will come from the failed kingdom of Israel.

After the reign of Kings David and Solomon, the kingdom of Israel splits, each side collapses and caves in because of moral decay and rebellion against God. Finally, one side is destroyed by Babylon, the other by the Assyrians. Isaiah's vision cast them as a forest laid to waste. The rings of their history exposed, revealing cycle after cycle of disobedience and stubborn-hearted sin.

But in the midst of the destruction, there is one flicker of hope. A shock of green in the wasteland. From the broken stump of Jesse, the father of David, there is a shoot that will become the Branch that will bear new and lasting fruit. The family tree of David will persevere and reclaim the throne once again.

Trees are a prominent image all the way throughout Scripture. They are central to both the first garden and the new creation. And in this passage, it seems as if Isaiah's vision of a broken stump is meant to stand between those two ends, tying them together. It's like Isaiah is reading a scroll that stretches from Genesis to Revelation. He is caught between a memory of what was and a vision of what is to come. He is, in a sense, remembering the future.

And this is what he sees: the Shoot is rising. The wasteland is not forever. The wait will soon be over. And when this long-awaited King arrives, he will bring with him a restoration of Eden. When his kingdom comes, enemies will be reconciled and creation will be healed. In the established reign of our Prince of Peace, the wild and dangerous wolf will lie down with the gentle lamb. And a little child will lead us into the arms of our Father forever.

From the stump of Jesse comes the Righteous Branch of David. And this Anointed Shepherd King, emerging from David's line and born in David's town, will defeat the giants of sin and death with the unlikely weapon of cross and blood.

The language of Isaiah is stirring. The beauty is captivating. But this is more than poetry. It's prophecy. And prophecy cuts through the page and across time and space and into the everyday. Which sparks the questions . . .

The Prayer

Prince of Peace, reconcile the impossible divisions that still exist in my life. Make my life look like your kingdom.

The Questions

- What will this reign of the King look like in my life? I'm happy that the wolf and lamb will work things out, but what does this mean for my home, my relationships, my anxiety, my mental and emotional and physical and spiritual health?
- Where do you see the Shoot pushing up from broken places?
- What does it look like when the Branch starts to bear his fruit in my life? What is changing in me because of his reign?

AND THE WORD BECAME FLESH,
AND MADE HIS DWELLING AMONG US.

Once and Future Kingdom

20

MARK 1:1 | The beginning of the good news about Jesus the Messiah, the Son of God . . .

Consider This

Unlike Matthew and Luke, the Gospel of Mark does not give us a birth narrative for Jesus. But he does begin with . . .

The beginning: All of Israel's past hope is culminating in the arrival of Jesus. In the following verse, the writer quotes an ancient prophecy from Isaiah, linking Jesus to the fulfillment of Israel's history. Yet Mark makes it clear that this is only the start of a brand-new future. This is a message to every other empire of the world that this Jesus movement may look like a tiny mark on the timeline of global events, but this story is larger than the world itself. And the scope of the human narrative so far has been building up to this. Now we are at the beginning.

Of the good news: To us today, this term is loaded with religious significance, and it should be. But it was not always that way. In the earliest days of Christianity, this was already a familiar phrase in the culture because it was used by the Roman Empire to describe a proclamation from Caesar. *"Good news! Caesar reigns and he is bringing peace!"* But Mark employs the term in a subversive and provocative way, declaring that the message of Jesus is the true good news for all people and Caesar's so-called "gospel" is a weak and empty parody of the real thing.

About Jesus the Messiah: Messiah is a title with roots in the Hebrew language, meaning "Anointed One." Echoing the story of David, the unlikely shepherd boy who was anointed king by the prophet Samuel, the people of Israel were awaiting another anointed King, a Son of David, to come and take his rightful place on the throne of Israel. For Mark to declare Jesus as that King would have been heresy to the Jewish religious establishment and treason to the oppressive Roman government. But the holy cannot be heresy. Truth is not treason.

The Son of God: Not only is Mark naming Jesus as the Son of David, but he takes the radical and scandalous step of calling him the Son of God. Yet again, this moves beyond our religious understanding of the language and has a political edge to it. Forty years before the birth of Jesus, Julius Caesar died. It was said that a comet was seen streaking through the sky at his death, and the legend was sold that this was a sign that Julius Caesar was now a divine figure. That would make his heir and adopted son, Caesar Augustus, the "son of a god." He demanded not only allegiance as a political leader, but worship as a divine leader. Mark's opening confession stands in defiant resistance, declaring that Jesus is the only true Son of the only true God.

The true King Jesus has come to establish his true kingdom, once and future, now and forever. And this mustard seed of a movement will go on to infiltrate the mighty Roman Empire, outlasting and outpacing, and reaching further than Augustus could have ever imagined with its revolutionary holy love.

The Prayer

King Jesus, we declare that our allegiance and affections belong to you. Let your unrivaled reign be seen in our lives.

The Questions

- How is the message of Jesus good news for you today?
- What corner of your life needs to be surrendered to his reign?

AND THE WORD BECAME FLESH,
AND MADE HIS DWELLING AMONG US.

21 Rebellion

LUKE 1:34–38 | "How will this be," Mary asked the angel, "since I am a virgin?"

The angel answered, "The Holy Spirit will come on you, and the power of the Most High will overshadow you. So the holy one to be born will be called the Son of God. Even Elizabeth your relative is going to have a child in her old age, and she who was said to be unable to conceive is in her sixth month. For no word from God will ever fail."

"I am the Lord's servant," Mary answered. "May your word to me be fulfilled." Then the angel left her.

Consider This

The name "Mary" can mean rebellion.

That's not an idea we normally associate with the Virgin Mary. We think of her as a stained-glass saint, one dimensional icon of holiness, prized role in the annual children's program.

Truth be told, we don't often think of her at all until it's time to unpack the nativity set again. Our tradition protested against the abuses of the papal institution and sought to reform the church in the image of its radical beginnings. So we tend to shy away from focusing on Mary at all out of fear of past misconceptions. But this is to our own great loss. Through this humble woman from a backwoods village, far out of the sphere of power, the Almighty draws near to us. As the baby kicks in her womb, empires tremble and a rebellion—yes, rebellion—is set in motion.

In today's passage, Mary is greeted by the impossibly good news that she will conceive the long-awaited hope of Israel. Even though she can't understand how this will happen through a virgin, she defies her doubt and responds with trust.

Mary's response in Nazareth stands in direct contrast to Eve's response in the garden. Faced with that first temptation, Eve's response of doubt leads to insurrection. Mary's response of trust leads to surrender. Eve is tempted to see herself as the Lord's equal. Mary responds, "I am the Lord's servant." Eve is tempted to doubt the words of God. Mary responds, "May your word to me be fulfilled."

In Advent, Mary launches the counter-rebellion against sin and death through this radical act of trust. The Way of Jesus is, in fact, just that. It's a holy rebellion against the way things are. It embodies the culture of a different kind of kingdom that threatens to upend the conventional order of things and usher in the customs of heaven on earth.

Still uncomfortable with the word *rebellion*? Then consider this as well: In the museum of the Bible located in Washington, DC, there is a popular exhibit known as the "Slave Bible." That thought alone should pierce your heart. But it gets worse. This English translation from the 1800s was specifically designed for the conversion of slaves to Christianity and to assist in their education. But in order to protect the status quo power dynamics of the plantation, this version was heavily edited. The goal being to remove any reference that might incite rebellion or awaken a longing for liberation. As you might expect, the end result was a Bible hardly recognizable.

According to the associate curator of the exhibit, there are 1,189 chapters in a standard Protestant Bible. This one contains 232—half of the New Testament is missing, and 90 percent of the Old Testament is missing.

Because across every page is a story that incites rebellion and awakens a longing for liberation. And now, as waiting becomes arrival, the Author of this story is stepping into it to become the Protagonist.

And like Mary, we delight in this impossibly good news. And we echo, "May it be to your servants as you have said."

The Prayer

Prince of Peace, reconcile the impossible divisions that still exist in my life. Make my life look like your kingdom.

The Questions

- Does your life look like a rebellion against sin, injustice, oppression, racism, hate? Or are you propping up the status quo?
- What is one way your life would change if you joined his rebellion?
- What act of radical trust is Jesus asking of you today?

AND THE WORD BECAME FLESH,
AND MADE HIS DWELLING AMONG US.

Five Minutes BC

MATTHEW 1:18–21 | This is how the birth of Jesus the Messiah came about: His mother Mary was pledged to be married to Joseph, but before they came together, she was found to be pregnant through the Holy Spirit. Because Joseph her husband was faithful to the law, and yet did not want to expose her to public disgrace, he had in mind to divorce her quietly.

But after he had considered this, an angel of the Lord appeared to him in a dream and said, "Joseph son of David, do not be afraid to take Mary home as your wife, because what is conceived in her is from the Holy Spirit. She will give birth to a son, and you are to give him the name Jesus, because he will save his people from their sins."

Consider This

This passage marks the exact moment when Joseph's life was changed forever. And ours along with it. It's not when Mary broke the news. It's not when he made the decision to quietly protect her honor. It's not when he slipped into the dream or saw the angel appear. All of these are important but they aren't the pivot. The story turns on a single word. A single name, to be exact. "She will give birth to a son, and you are to give him the name Jesus, because he will save his people from their sins."

Jesus. What a beautiful name. The history of the world hangs on this name. Martyrs have laid down their lives for it. Sinners have found forgiveness in it. Sick have found healing in it. Dead have been called into life by it. Slaves have found freedom through it. Addicts have found restoration in it. Doubters have found their faith in it. Scholars have searched layer after layer of mysterious truth and still can't find the end of it. And at the mention of this name, hell shakes and hearts sing and heaven opens wide its gates.

There is something irresistible about this name and the life that fills it up. The whole story turns in this moment when his name is introduced. Indeed, every name before has been pointing to his. Adam, Noah, Abraham, Moses, David. Each covenant a chapter teaching us to long for all things to be completed in him.

Unlike those Old Testament narratives, I've noticed that the Gospels aren't very concerned with character development. Most individuals are not given much of a backstory. Yes, we get Joseph's genealogy as a recap of the Old Testament journey. But that is about Jesus. We aren't actually told much about Joseph. We aren't given any background on Mary. The same will happen later with Jesus' disciples and the people that he encounters through his ministry. In the Gospels we seem to pick up everyone's story somewhere around Five Minutes BC. We don't encounter them until they are about to encounter Jesus.

That's because the story is never about them. The Story begins when Jesus steps into it. The same is true for you. Who you were, where you were, what you were before Jesus is not the story. Your story began when Jesus stepped into it. And this Author has always been crafting the script and bending the arc and redeeming the subplots to prepare for this entrance.

As we edge ever closer to the moment of his arrival, this name starts to form on our lips and take root in our souls and lay claim to our stories. He will be called Jesus, because he will save his people from their sins.

The Prayer

Jesus, the name above all names. There is no better sound in our ears or on our tongues. Your name is true to its meaning. You have saved us. We thank you. And we love you.

The Questions

- What does the name of Jesus mean to you?
- How has your life been changed by it?

AND THE WORD BECAME FLESH,
AND MADE HIS DWELLING AMONG US.

23 Where Is God?

MATTHEW 1:22–25 | All this took place to fulfill what the Lord had said through the prophet: "The virgin will conceive and give birth to a son, and they will call him Immanuel" (which means "God with us").

When Joseph woke up, he did what the angel of the Lord had commanded him and took Mary home as his wife. But he did not consummate their marriage until she gave birth to a son. And he gave him the name Jesus.

Consider This

As we anticipate the arrival of Jesus, we begin by reminding ourselves of how desperately we needed a Savior in the first place. As we celebrate the season of light, we remember that he found us in the darkness. As we rejoice in our redemption and hope in Jesus, we remember how hopeless we are without him.

When tragedy strikes, we are reminded of this desperation in ways that are too deep for words. What words we can grab hold of take shape as questions. Why me? Why her? Who is safe? What is sacred? Where can we hide that is off-limits to evil?

We light the Peace candle in our Advent wreath and wonder if there was even any sense in doing so. Is there any flicker of peace left in this world?

And perhaps the most important question of all: Where is God in this?

Perhaps many of you find this question all too familiar this year as you wrestle with grief and sorrow in a season so connected with joy. The longing of Advent and the hope of Christmas offer an unexpected answer: God is with us. He is not distant from the pain and heartache of this broken world. Instead, in the mystery of the incarnation, he enters into it. God becomes a victim of violence, a target of tragedy. He comes into this violent and broken world as a vulnerable and breakable child.

We need this good news now. And Joseph needed this good news then. As Joseph's entire world is caving in on him, reeling from this revelation that Mary is expecting a child that does not belong to him, sorting through the broken fragments of betrayal and public shame and private confusion, he receives this word: do not be afraid. God is with you.

The prophecy referenced here is originally spoken centuries before, in Isaiah 7. And it comes through Isaiah to King Ahaz in a moment of fear and despair. The people are surrounded and threatened from every side. The enemy is closing in. They need a miracle. And into this, Isaiah says that God's strategy for your deliverance, your security, your joy, your deepest satisfaction, your peace, your hope, your future, your here and your now is this: the Lord himself will give you a sign. God with us.

Where is God when our world comes undone? The manger tells us he is with us. The manger tells us he enters into our broken world to be broken by it—and so, to redeem it. The manger tells us that into this deep and despairing darkness a Light is dawning. The manger tells us to look again, in full anticipation of his second Advent, when Jesus our hope will return to heal every hurt, to bind up the brokenhearted, and wipe every tear from our eyes. He will swallow up tragedy in a tide of swelling redemption and enduring hope. Behold, the strategy of God.

The Prayer

God with us, enter into our tragedy and pain with your healing presence.

The Questions

- How is "God with us" good news in your life?
- Where have you found him amidst the broken places?
- How has he shown up in your tragedies?

> AND THE WORD BECAME FLESH,
> AND MADE HIS DWELLING AMONG US.

24 Christmas Eve

LUKE 2:8–12 | And there were shepherds living out in the fields nearby, keeping watch over their flocks at night. An angel of the Lord appeared to them, and the glory of the Lord shone around them, and they were terrified. But the angel said to them, "Do not be afraid. I bring you good news that will cause great joy for all the people. Today in the town of David a Savior has been born to you; he is the Messiah, the Lord. This will be a sign to you: You will find a baby wrapped in cloths and lying in a manger."

Consider This

We've been waiting. We've been longing. And now, the culmination of Advent. He is here.

Today, I'm struck by the timing of his arrival. Not the age in history or season of the year. But the time of day, the hour at which it occurs. This arrival takes place at night. These are the only two words of timing that we are given: "at night." In the thick of night is where the Light finds us.

One of the most persistent symbols of Christmas is the candle. Sure, we hang strings of bulbs on Christmas trees. We display our Moravian stars. And some of us turn our homes into flashing and blinking monstrosities visible from space. But through all of this, the candle shines brightest as the symbol of our journey of hope, joy, peace, and love.

All around the world tonight, Christians are gathering in cathedrals and stadiums and homes and caves and palaces and war-torn battlefields and a little movie theater. And in all of these places and more, Christians are singing songs and reading this story by simple candle light.

A reminder that the Light has come. And he chooses to show up in the middle of darkness, in the unexpectedly small and simple ways. A stubborn flicker of resistance, a defiant spark of hope. Passed from one person to the next, this Light advances and the darkness is forced into retreat, with no place left to hide.

And no matter how much the darkness howls and threatens and fights to snuff it out, the darkness has not, and will not, overcome it. The people living in darkness have seen a great Light. On those living in the valley of the shadows, the Light has dawned. After the long night of waiting, the Morning himself has arrived at last. And Eve's weeping gives way to Mary's song. We raise our candles and voices together and sing along. "Joy to the World, the Lord is come! Let earth receive her King."

The Prayer

Light of the world, we have been waiting for the morning. We are waking up to find it more than we could have dreamed.

The Questions
- How has the light of Jesus overcome the darkness in this past year?
- Whom has he used to shine into your life this year?
- What is one thing you are grateful for about the year behind you?

AND THE WORD BECAME FLESH,
AND MADE HIS DWELLING AMONG US.

Small Moments

25

LUKE 2:1–7 | In those days Caesar Augustus issued a decree that a census should be taken of the entire Roman world. (This was the first census that took place while Quirinius was governor of Syria.) And everyone went to their own town to register.

So Joseph also went up from the town of Nazareth in Galilee to Judea, to Bethlehem the town of David, because he belonged to the house and line of David. He went there to register with Mary, who was pledged to be married to him and was expecting a child. While they were there, the time came for the baby to be born, and she gave birth to her firstborn, a son. She wrapped him in cloths and placed him in a manger, because there was no guest room available for them.

Consider This

This is a small moment, when we hold our breath
As the fate of the world stands at a tipping point.
Where ancient truth meets wonder.
Where the promise you saw coming catches you by surprise.
Where the waiting gives way to fulfillment.
Where certainty is filled with mystery and mystery is anchored in certainty.
This is the moment
When seas split open and a way is made.

When the impossible comes within reach.
When giants start to stumble.
When chains break and slaves walk free.
When empires flinch and a kingdom rises.
This is the moment
When eyes open.
When lips sing.
When legs dance.
When hearts heal.
This is the moment
Where the God
Of Abraham and Isaac
Of Moses and Elijah
Of David and Jesse
Becomes the God
Of Mary and Joseph
Of you and me.
This is the moment
When the God
Of fire and flood
Of holiness and love
Of justice and mercy
Of miracle and might
Becomes flesh and blood.
This is the moment of Immanuel—God with us.
When the one who fills up every corner of existence
Is now cradled in a manger.

When dawn overcomes the night.
When love overthrows sin.
When a baby takes his first breath
And gives creation a second chance.

The Prayer

Jesus, we welcome your arrival at last! The Story is yours.

The Questions

- Look back over our Advent journey together. What stands out most to you?
- What words of welcome do you have for Jesus today?

> AND THE WORD BECAME FLESH,
> AND MADE HIS DWELLING AMONG US.

Revelation

26

SONG OF SOLOMON 2:10–13 | My beloved spoke and said to me: "Arise, my darling, my beautiful one, and come with me. See! The winter is past; the rains are over and gone. Flowers appear on the earth; the season of singing has come, the cooing of doves is heard in our land. The fig tree forms its early fruit; the blossoming vines spread their fragrance. Arise, come, my darling; my beautiful one, come with me."

Consider This

Today continues the season of what's known in the liturgical calendar as *Christmastide* (this is the "second day of Christmas"). This short period moves us on through the new year and to Epiphany on January 6. Epiphany essentially means "manifestation." When the ineffable is made tangible, we call that a manifestation. What previously proved elusive is suddenly brought close. We often equate an epiphany with a sudden flash of insight, but that understanding misses the tangible nature of a genuine epiphany. We experience an epiphany, not only when we see things from a fresh perspective, but when we physically behold a reality that wasn't there just a moment ago.

We have just come through the longer season of Advent, which is a season of waiting and anticipation. With the physical birth of Jesus, we transition now into a posture of beholding. The wait is over. In the bleakness of winter we look upon the one who is the hope of all nations. The birth of Jesus transforms reality from the inside out. Our long nights of grief are given a sense of meaning. Our losses are not undone, but begin to be seen as instruments of redemption that have hewn away our pride, and created space for compassion. With the arrival of Jesus, none of our circumstances are structurally altered, yet all things are now permeated by a primal light, and the shattered fragments have been brought back together. Jesus may not give us all of the answers, but he meets a deeper need by giving us a way to live in the face of uncertainty.

In this sense, Epiphany is not so much a season as it is a person. Jesus is the Epiphany. He is not the revealer. He is the revelation itself. In the lowliness of his birth, and in the radical submission of his ministry, Jesus makes manifest the character of God. He is the radiant, once-and-for-all reminder of God's unswerving commitment to his creation, and he gives us hope enough to be holy.

The Prayer

Thank you, Father, for hearing the deepest cry of our heart, and for responding by sending Jesus into our midst.

The Questions

- Can you hear the voice of the Beloved calling out to you in your darkness? What is he saying?
- What do the lowly conditions of Jesus' birth reveal to you about his willingness to meet you where you are?

AND THE WORD BECAME FLESH,
AND MADE HIS DWELLING AMONG US.

Ripple Effect

27

ISAIAH 11:5–9 | Righteousness will be his belt and faithfulness the sash around his waist. The wolf will live with the lamb, the leopard will lie down with the goat, the calf and the lion and the yearling together; and a little child will lead them. The cow will feed with the bear, their young will lie down together, and the lion will eat straw like the ox. The infant will play near the cobra's den, and the young child will put its hand into the viper's nest. They will neither harm nor destroy on all my holy mountain, for the earth will be filled with the knowledge of the LORD as the waters cover the sea.

Consider This

For all of the beauty of this passage, we are often guilty of removing it from its natural context. The prophet is not merely painting a hopeful image for an idealized future. He is speaking words of hope in the face of unrelenting exile. His people were in the throes of Babylonian exile; removed from their homes, removed from their streets, and perhaps, most significantly, estranged from their place of worship. Yet notice how universal and comprehensive his vision proves to be! It is not merely of a rebuilt temple that he speaks. He speaks instead of a return to the way things were. His words depict Eden, yet an Eden that has been enhanced through the process of deep redemption. It is hard for us to imagine Isaiah's ideal world ever being born into reality. Harder still for his original hearers to take him seriously as they lived as strangers in a pagan land, while all they held sacred lay in a pile of burnt rubble.

Isaiah 11 is often spoken of as a vision of the messianic kingdom; the earthly reign of the Messiah, which is to be marked by universal wholeness. It is a future reality that we as Christians are currently longing for . . . at least in theory. Yet this prophecy holds an important place for us in the here and now. The much-anticipated Messiah has been born in the most humble of circumstances. While we await his climactic return, we must yet remember that his birth is the guarantee of things to come.

When you drop a pebble into a pond, it may take a while for the ripples to work their way to the shore. But . . . the pebble has been dropped. The ripples arriving at the shore is an inevitability. With the birth of Jesus, the pebble has been dropped. The healing of the cosmos is now inevitable. At this very moment, the ripples are rapidly making their way to the shore. Jesus has already done everything that needs to be done. There are no missing ingredients. All that remains is for us, as his followers, to hasten the restoration of all things by prayer and obedience. His long-awaited arrival has awakened within us an even deeper yearning for his imminent return.

The Prayer

Creator and Sustainer of all that is, renew within us a hunger for the completion of your plan.

The Questions

- Look around you. Can you see any ripples? Any indication that the restoration is already underway?

- How does the birth of Jesus give you hope for today and not just for the distant future?

> AND THE WORD BECAME FLESH,
> AND MADE HIS DWELLING AMONG US.

28 The One of Peace

MICAH 5:4–5 NRSV | And he shall stand and feed his flock in the strength of the LORD, in the majesty of the name of the LORD his God. And they shall live secure, for now he shall be great to the ends of the earth; and he shall be the one of peace.

Consider This

In this passage, we find another prophetic promise of the coming messianic kingdom. This time it's from Micah, likely a younger contemporary of Isaiah. Although there are similarities of deep significance, Micah's forecast differs from the vision of Isaiah 11:5–9 in one important way. It tells us exactly what kind of person this Messiah will be. As Micah tells it, "He will be the one of peace." So the ultimate promise is not just of a peaceful kingdom, but of a peaceful King.

Jesus is the "one of peace." He came preaching a message of peace, and he fully embodied the words that he spoke. To pick one example, Jesus' discourse in Luke 6 may be the most unflinching articulation of non-violence on record. His ethic of peace was not the result of a mere political orientation, but of a deep encounter with his Abba. Jesus spoke the truth, come what may, because he trusted his Source. He refused to incite violence because he knew that the one who sees all would ultimately right every wrong. He encouraged his followers to have their own encounter, in the hopes that they might reach a similar conclusion. We all rest in the hands of a benevolent God who is more than happy to take care of us. Therefore, we need not expend so much energy trying to take care of ourselves. If the Essence of Existence is actively bringing about the balance of all things, then revenge is a waste of time.

The prophecy in Micah 5 actually begins in chapter 4, where the prophet boldly proclaims that, "They shall study war no more" (4:3) in the coming reign of the Messiah. An end to war is a central theme in a great many messianic prophecies. And now we are reminded again that the Messiah has already arrived . . . in the flesh. In his birth and subsequent life, Jesus has already brought peace. The prevalence of war in our world is an indication of how few of us have actually surrendered to the way of Jesus, who is the ultimate manifestation of God's character. As we more deeply surrender ourselves to this unprecedented manifestation, I feel that we will find ourselves laying down our weapons and choosing our words with greater wisdom.

The Prayer

God of peace, you have revealed yourself most perfectly through Jesus. Help us, by way of your Holy Spirit, to follow his example in becoming a people of peace.

The Questions

- There is a direct connection between inner peace and outer peace. Is there an inner restlessness in your life? How is it manifesting in outward hostility?
- Are you engaged in any daily practices that might help to cultivate peace in your relationships?

AND THE WORD BECAME FLESH,
AND MADE HIS DWELLING AMONG US.

29 Border Crossing

MATTHEW 2:1–6 | After Jesus was born in Bethlehem in Judea, during the time of King Herod, Magi from the east came to Jerusalem and asked, "Where is the one who has been born king of the Jews? We saw his star when it rose and have come to worship him."

When King Herod heard this, he was disturbed, and all Jerusalem with him. When he had called together all the people's chief priests and teachers of the law, he asked them where the Messiah was to be born. "In Bethlehem in Judea," they replied, "for this is what the prophet has written:

"'But you, Bethlehem, in the land of Judah, are by no means least among the rulers of Judah; for out of you will come a ruler who will shepherd my people Israel.'"

Consider This

The circumstances surrounding the birth of the Christ-Child have much to say about what kind of person he would be. Where he was born, and to whom, hint at the earthiness and humility of his future ministry. And what about the folks who were there to greet him? Jesus was welcomed into the world by shepherds and pagans. The facts surrounding these wise men, or magi, are murky at best. We are not told who they represented, nor are we informed as to the exact nature of their profession. We do know where they came from, and we do know what they came to do. They came from the East.

In the first century, nearly everything east of Jerusalem belonged to the Parthian Empire, within which a multitude of religions were tolerated. Whichever of these the wise men practiced, they were most certainly not Jews! Their religion was different. Their culture was different. Everything about them was different. Yet, they leave everything behind to enter into the presence of Jesus. They were compelled to pay him homage. As the narrative in Matthew 2 continues, we are told that the wise men returned to their home country, but that they did so by way of a different route. We are told that they did so to avoid another encounter with Herod. What is the deeper meaning of this? I perceive it as an indication that they returned to their native place, and even to their former practices, yet in a fundamentally altered state due to their encounter with the Messiah.

This story is not just a foretelling of things to come. What we have here is a full disclosure of Jesus' DNA. This is who

Jesus is, drawing people like a magnet with an alarming disregard for the arbitrary boundaries that seem so sacred to the rest of us. He didn't care that they came from a distant land. He didn't care that they brought cultural and religious baggage along with their gifts. I propose that these men weren't just drawn westward by a distant star, but by the love that emanated from the heart of the newborn King. Before he had even learned to walk, he was already welcoming the stranger.

The Prayer

Creator God, through the work of Jesus, you invite everyone to the table. Cultivate within us a spirit of hospitality and a willingness to lose friends in our resolve to welcome the stranger.

The Questions

- Examine your relationships. Have you allowed a fear of the other to birth a spirit of exclusion?
- How many of your friends look or believe differently than you?

AND THE WORD BECAME FLESH,
AND MADE HIS DWELLING AMONG US.

Simeon's Ecstasy

LUKE 2:25–32 | Now there was a man in Jerusalem called Simeon, who was righteous and devout. He was waiting for the consolation of Israel, and the Holy Spirit was on him. It had been revealed to him by the Holy Spirit that he would not die before he had seen the Lord's Messiah. Moved by the Spirit, he went into the temple courts. When the parents brought in the child Jesus to do for him what the custom of the Law required, Simeon took him in his arms and praised God, saying:

"Sovereign Lord, as you have promised, you may now dismiss your servant in peace. For my eyes have seen your salvation, which you have prepared in the sight of all nations: a light for revelation to the Gentiles and the glory of your people Israel."

Consider This

I imagine Simeon's prayer could have continued something like this:

"Yahweh, you have proven yourself as a faithful, ever-present, and self-giving Master. I have been your servant for these many years, and it has been the pleasure of my life. Long ago the bright fire of your Spirit came to consume me. Since then, my eyes have looked in every direction for a single reality. You have filled my heart with a love for your Presence, and you have broken it over the plight of my people, who were your people first. You have given me few words with which to console them. My gifts from you were not words for your people, but tears for your people. I have offered you my mouth to speak through, but you preferred to weep through my eyes. I have been a man of prayer, and I have been a man of fasting. Even in my eating, I have never lost my longing for the Great Fulfillment.

"From the time that I became a man, my life has been as a single prostration before you. I am a man, and as such, I am subject to the same temptations as other men. I have dropped my shoulders and allowed the energy of my natural impulses to wash over me. I have offered no resistance, yet I have succumbed to no indulgence. I have felt the separation of heaven and earth within my body, and now my eyes at last fall upon the agent of connection . . . the one by whom you hold all things together. And now all things will be more held together than ever before. The tension of separation that I have carried like a brother in the center of my chest is finally released. There is no need for me to see anything else. Take me now, while my gratitude exceeds my expectations."

The Prayer

Creator and Sustainer, remind us that you act only in response to our longing. Intensify our longing for that which is real, and birth in us an intolerance for anything less.

The Questions

- In an ultra-materialistic society, how do you keep your most sacred longings alive?

- Simeon risked humiliation in identifying a baby as the embodied hope of his people, and he did so in public. When you see Jesus, are you willing to speak it?

> AND THE WORD BECAME FLESH,
> AND MADE HIS DWELLING AMONG US.

Awareness and Spiritual Practice | 31

LUKE 2:36–38 | There was also a prophet, Anna, the daughter of Penuel, of the tribe of Asher. She was very old; she had lived with her husband seven years after her marriage, and then was a widow until she was eighty-four. She never left the temple but worshiped night and day, fasting and praying. Coming up to them at that very moment, she gave thanks to God and spoke about the child to all who were looking forward to the redemption of Jerusalem.

Consider This

Simeon is referred to as a righteous and devout man, who had eagerly awaited the messianic fulfillment. He lays eyes upon Jesus and proceeds to praise the God who sent him and to speak words of encouragement to Mary and Joseph. Anna was no doubt righteous and devout as well, but she is specifically referred to as a prophet. Seeing Jesus puts her directly into preaching mode. She does pause to give praise where praise is due, but spreading the good news to anyone who would listen seemed to be her most urgent priority.

While acknowledging the difference in self-expression, I suspect that it was a set of shared attributes that opened both sets of eyes to the same reality. In Simeon and Anna, we have two individuals whose lives were permeated by spiritual practice. Calling Simeon "righteous and devout" certainly implies a life of discipline and devotion. With Anna, the description is more explicit. In a span of three verses, we are told that she is devoted to prayer, fasting, and chastity. She recognized Jesus and proclaimed it to the masses because she was a prophet. But to what do we attribute her prophetic gifting? Did it have anything to do with her holy lifestyle?

I suggest that praise and prophetic speech flow as a result of revelation. Anna's ascetic lifestyle heightened her spiritual senses, which allowed her to receive revelation. The revelation itself served as a catalyst for prophetic speech. So maybe God doesn't only speak to prophets. Maybe prophets are prophets, not because God exclusively speaks to them, but because they choose to listen to what God is, in fact, saying to everyone.

The Prayer

Spirit of the living God, challenge us in our apathy and forge us into a community of prophets.

The Questions

- Are prayer and fasting a significant part of your devotional life?
- Do you sense these disciplines as channels of grace and revelation or as compulsory obligations?

AND THE WORD BECAME FLESH,
AND MADE HIS DWELLING AMONG US.

Incarnation

32

JOHN 1:14–18 | The Word became flesh and made his dwelling among us. We have seen his glory, the glory of the one and only Son, who came from the Father, full of grace and truth.

(John testified concerning him. He cried out, saying, "This is the one I spoke about when I said, 'He who comes after me has surpassed me because he was before me.'") Out of his fullness we have all received grace in place of grace already given. For the law was given through Moses; grace and truth came through Jesus Christ. No one has ever seen God, but the one and only Son, who is himself God and is in closest relationship with the Father, has made him known.

Consider This

I'm not sure that we would have much of a philosophy of the incarnation were it not for the first chapter of John.

This idea of God revealing himself through a human vessel is really quite radical. Our inclination is often to view God as distant; far removed from the intricate details of his creation. The reality of the incarnation as it is expressed through John speaks a much better word.

Saint Athanasius must have had the words of John resonating within his mind when he wrote his classic work *On the Incarnation of the Word*. In my view, Athanasius gives the most profound and concise explanation of the incarnation when he says, "God became what we are, so that we might become what he is." This is a simple explication of the Orthodox notion of *theosis*, which is the process by which we become like God by way of union with him. We can be made like God in character. Through the experience of union with him, we can come to love what he loves. His values become our values and his opinions become our opinions. Jesus shows what it looks like for a human to be perfectly united with the Source—living with God in an unbroken bond of intimacy that cannot help but produce a lifestyle of radical obedience. Shockingly, Jesus invites us into this same reality. He invites us into union. When we surrender to Jesus and become possessed by his Spirit, we too become incarnations. I believe this is what is implied in 2 Peter 1:4, where we are encouraged to "participate in the divine nature." He became what we are, that we might become what he is. I would add . . . if we never get around to becoming what he is, then there was really no point in him becoming what we are.

The Prayer

Creator and Sustainer of all that is, thank you for shining your light so brightly through Jesus. May his intimacy with you become our intimacy with you. May your thoughts become our thoughts, and may your ways become our ways.

The Questions

- Do you desire to move more deeply into this unbroken union with God?
- What barriers hinder this lifestyle of radical obedience?

AND THE WORD BECAME FLESH,
AND MADE HIS DWELLING AMONG US.

Jesus and the Temple   33

LUKE 2:46–50 | After three days they found him in the temple courts, sitting among the teachers, listening to them and asking them questions. Everyone who heard him was amazed at his understanding and his answers. When his parents saw him, they were astonished. His mother said to him, "Son, why have you treated us like this? Your father and I have been anxiously searching for you."

"Why were you searching for me?" he asked. "Didn't you know I had to be in my Father's house?" But they did not understand what he was saying to them.

Consider This

It is my opinion that Jesus lived the most remarkable life that has ever been lived. Nearly everything that we know about this life comes to us through the Gospel accounts. We have a substantial amount of information regarding his brief but truly awesome ministry. We have a few stories regarding his infancy. Of his childhood, we have only this single story from Luke 2. It's quite a story though. The boy Jesus has apparently spent the better part of several days sitting among the scholars in the temple. He impressed them with his answers, but also asked questions and listened carefully to the replies. This was all done to the great bewilderment of his very concerned parents.

When I read this story of the twelve-year-old Jesus, sitting in humility and absorbing the wisdom of the sages, I can't help but flash-forward to a very different scene toward the end of Jesus' earthly life. This Jesus who sat contemplatively among the scholars of the temple would one day come unglued within the confines of that very same temple. I wonder if there were any folks who got to witness both events . . . if any of these teachers who were impressed by the dignified intelligence of this very special young man were also there when he started tossing tables and spilling coins. If so, they must have sincerely wondered what had happened to him.

I think these two temple events go together in a very important way. Putting them side by side, we see a Jesus who slowly internalized the religion of his people. He questioned it, he pondered it, and he applied himself to walking by its light. But over time, Jesus came to some radical conclusions. Some of these conclusions led him to make a rather sudden break with establishment Judaism. By the time that his official ministry began, Jesus had cast his lot with the prophets. His final incident in the temple was the culmination of this change. There were aspects of the temple system and of its oppressive hierarchy that Jesus flatly rejected, and he let everybody know it.

Like everyone, Jesus had to get there in his own way and in his own time. But when he got there, it was a sight to behold. As it has been said, Jesus was more than a prophet, but he was never less than a prophet. He followed in the footsteps of the prophets, and yet fulfilled their words at the same time. His words and his actions were perfectly on time, because he *took* his time. His most radical actions emerged from a deeply cultivated disposition of inquisitive humility.

The Prayer
Make us like Jesus.

The Questions
- Is it your tendency to lash out before listening? How can you cultivate Jesus' pattern of listening long before lashing, of weeping before whipping?
- If listening and learning from others come naturally for you, are you willing to speak plainly when the moment arrives?

AND THE WORD BECAME FLESH,
AND MADE HIS DWELLING AMONG US.

34 | Death and Resurrection

MATTHEW 3:13–16 | Then Jesus came from Galilee to the Jordan to be baptized by John. But John tried to deter him, saying, "I need to be baptized by you, and do you come to me?"

Jesus replied, "Let it be so now; it is proper for us to do this to fulfill all righteousness." Then John consented.

As soon as Jesus was baptized, he went up out of the water. At that moment heaven was opened, and he saw the Spirit of God descending like a dove and alighting on him.

Consider This

The baptism of John is referred to in Acts 19 as a baptism of repentance, and that's how we normally think of baptism, as a public turning away from selfish living. But if baptism were only a matter of repentance, then there would have been no need for Jesus to be baptized, seeing as how he had no selfish past to renounce. Although baptism does normally imply repentance, I believe there is a deeper meaning to this ancient ritual. Baptism is first and foremost a ritual of submission and surrender. To put it plainly, letting another human being hold you under water is a profound expression of trust! When a person walks down into the waters of baptism, they are saying for the whole world to hear, "I surrender. I submit my will to the will of the one who upholds everything that he created. I will seek the good of the whole picture above my own self-interest, and I will sacrifice that which is temporal for the sake of that which is eternal." Taking a deep breath and yielding to the hands of another, trusting that you will reemerge from the water, is a potent symbol of the self-sacrifice that always leads to resurrection. For Jesus, it was also a foreshadowing of what was to take place in his ministry.

The death and rebirth that are symbolized by baptism can be seen throughout the life of Christ. From his first miracle, to the washing of his disciples' feet, to the ultimate miracle of Easter, it's one example after another of Jesus letting himself be taken under in total trust that he would be brought back up. All he did was die. All he did was rise again. In doing so, he sanctified the role of the servant for all time. He did a lot more than just that though. Jesus physically embodied the one truth that is currently holding the universe together; the truth that all life comes through death, and that all beauty comes through sacrifice. Jesus wasn't afraid to go under. He knew it was the only path to resurrection.

The Prayer

Giver of life, equip us with the courage to surrender. Help us to trust that your hands will bring us back up at the proper time.

The Questions

- What act of service are you afraid might take you under for good? Remember that redemption often follows a downward path, but that it always leads to life.

- What emotion or memory are you afraid might take you under for good? Sometimes the path of life can lead through painful valleys. It's always worth it.

AND THE WORD BECAME FLESH,
AND MADE HIS DWELLING AMONG US.

35 Spreading the Joy

JOHN 2:7–11 | Jesus said to the servants, "Fill the jars with water"; so they filled them to the brim.

Then he told them, "Now draw some out and take it to the master of the banquet."

They did so, and the master of the banquet tasted the water that had been turned into wine. He did not realize where it had come from, though the servants who had drawn the water knew. Then he called the bridegroom aside and said, "Everyone brings out the choice wine first and then the cheaper wine after the guests have had too much to drink; but you have saved the best till now."

What Jesus did here in Cana of Galilee was the first of the signs through which he revealed his glory; and his disciples believed in him.

Consider This

Here we have an account of Jesus' first miracle. For me at least, it is also his most confounding. I have heard a few decent explanations that may well be valid. My favorite take is that this sign was in fact Jesus' first healing, and a mass healing at that. The logic behind this perspective is that the water would have otherwise been undrinkable—that the bacteria-laden water of that time would have sickened the wedding guests had Jesus not turned it into wine. I have preached that one myself, but I'm honestly not totally convinced that it's a thing. Plus, I have to swallow my pride and acknowledge that Jesus was not as tee-totaling as myself, and that he may not have shared my negative bias toward alcoholic beverage.

Psalm 104 is a deeply inspiring hymn to the Creator, praising him for the wonder of his innumerable works. And right there in verse 15, the psalmist praises the Lord for bringing forth wine "that gladdens human hearts." In the Bible, wine stands as a versatile symbol, and it is sometimes used as a symbol of joy. Whether or not wine brings joy is beyond the scope of my experience, but I do know that Jesus liked to spread the joy. And, as long as folks weren't trying to attain joy at the expense of someone else's joy, Jesus himself was a joyful person.

On my refrigerator, I have a picture of the Laughing Jesus. The expression on his face reveals a deeply seated joy that has spontaneously sprung to the surface . . . a joy that employs the entire face in an urgent attempt to express itself. Jesus was *full* of joy. It was a joy that was rooted in his knowledge of the Father. He had submerged himself in his Father's kindness and he had come up laughing. Joy filled him to the point of overflowing and spilled onto everyone who came close to him—unless they were allergic. So I guess it wasn't about preventing dysentery any more than it was about advocating public drunkenness. It was about what it is always about; Jesus manifesting himself as God's Spirit-filled emissary, come to save us from sin and from sadness.

The Prayer

Giver of life and light, make us radiant with joy. Heal us at the root so that we can celebrate from the depths of our being.

The Questions

- When was the last time that you felt the medicinal effects of laughter?
- Does your understanding of the gospel give you freedom to celebrate?

AND THE WORD BECAME FLESH,
AND MADE HIS DWELLING AMONG US.

Wisdom in the Flesh

36

PROVERBS 8:27–32 NRSV | "When he established the heavens, I was there, when he drew a circle on the face of the deep, when he made firm the skies above, when he established the fountains of the deep, when he assigned to the sea its limit, so that the waters might not transgress his command, when he marked out the foundations of the earth, then I was beside him, like a master worker; and I was daily his delight, rejoicing before him always, rejoicing in his inhabited world and delighting in the human race.

And now, my children, listen to me; happy are those who keep my ways."

Consider This

Proverbs 8 gives us an eloquent expression of a universal reality. This universal reality, which is seen as the vessel of God's creative activity, has been called by many names. That's partly because its essence transcends conceptual boundaries. Solomon refers to this reality as "wisdom," but it's difficult for me to read this proverb and not think of Jesus. In these days between Christmas and Epiphany, we focus on Jesus as the earthly manifestation of a primordial reality. While we rightly look upon his earthly life as our divine pattern of obedience, we remember that his life didn't begin in the manger. He was with the Father from the beginning, joining with him in the process of creation. We can see Jesus just as clearly in Proverbs 8 as we can in John 1.

Jesus is at once the archetype of creation and the vessel through whom all things came to be. Colossians 1 tells us that the spiritual presence of Jesus is holding it all together. Subtracting the Spirit of Jesus from creation doesn't lead to despair. It leads to complete disintegration. Jesus is our teacher. Jesus is our healer. Yet he is above all else a walking symbol of our connection with God. He is a reminder of God's intense longing for intimacy and he opens the way for us to experience this intimacy for ourselves. He is the example, plus the energy to follow it. If we are wise, we will submit to his presence and we will seek to follow in his ways.

The Prayer

Open our eyes to the presence of Jesus within the created order. The reality of death and rebirth surrounds us, yet the awareness of Jesus eludes us. Give us eyes to see.

The Questions

- Where in creation do you see evidence of Jesus?
- What is the connection between the earthly Jesus and primordial wisdom? How does Jesus manifest this reality?

AND THE WORD BECAME FLESH,
AND MADE HIS DWELLING AMONG US.

The Song of Creation

37

PSALM 96:11–13 | Let the heavens rejoice, let the earth be glad; let the sea resound, and all that is in it. Let the fields be jubilant, and everything in them; let all of the trees of the forest sing for joy. Let all creation rejoice before the Lᴏʀᴅ, for he comes, he comes to judge the earth. He will judge the world in righteousness and the peoples in his faithfulness.

Consider This

Over the past twelve days, we have been celebrating how Yahweh manifested himself through Jesus—the Protagonist. As we bring this particular season of celebration to a close, we remember that the coming of Jesus as the long-awaited Messiah is not just good news for all people, it is good news for all creation. God has a plan for creation. He created all things out of a deep reservoir of love, and everything he created he declared as "good." God does not waste anything. He makes it perfectly clear in the Scriptures that his intention is the full restoration of the cosmos. There will be purification and renewal, but those are not the same as destruction.

We can sometimes become hyper-focused on God's intention to save individual souls and forget that his plan is comprehensive; it includes us as individuals, but it's not about us as individuals. It's about the piecing back together of the whole picture, of which we are a part. For this reason, Psalm 96 depicts all of creation rejoicing at the coming of the

Lord. As the connector of heaven and earth, Jesus is the one that even the trees long to see, and at the sight of him, they cannot hide their relief. In his birth and life, Jesus set into motion the mending of all things. In his imminent return, he will set the seal on all that the prophets have spoken. God will send his Chosen One to heal all that ails us. He will do so when he chooses, yet it is not for us to stand by passively. By living a holy life, we can hasten the fulfillment of Psalm 96. We undermine the nature of things through wastefulness and self-indulgence. Holiness implies simplicity, and simplicity is medicine for all that lives.

The Prayer

Close the gap between heaven and earth. Forgive us for any role that we have played in producing and maintaining the schism that currently exists. With Jesus as our impulse, reconnect us with the land, and reconnect us with our neighbors.

The Questions

- Have you experienced creation as a means of grace?
- Can you find time in the next few days to take a slow walk in the woods?

AND THE WORD BECAME FLESH,
AND MADE HIS DWELLING AMONG US.